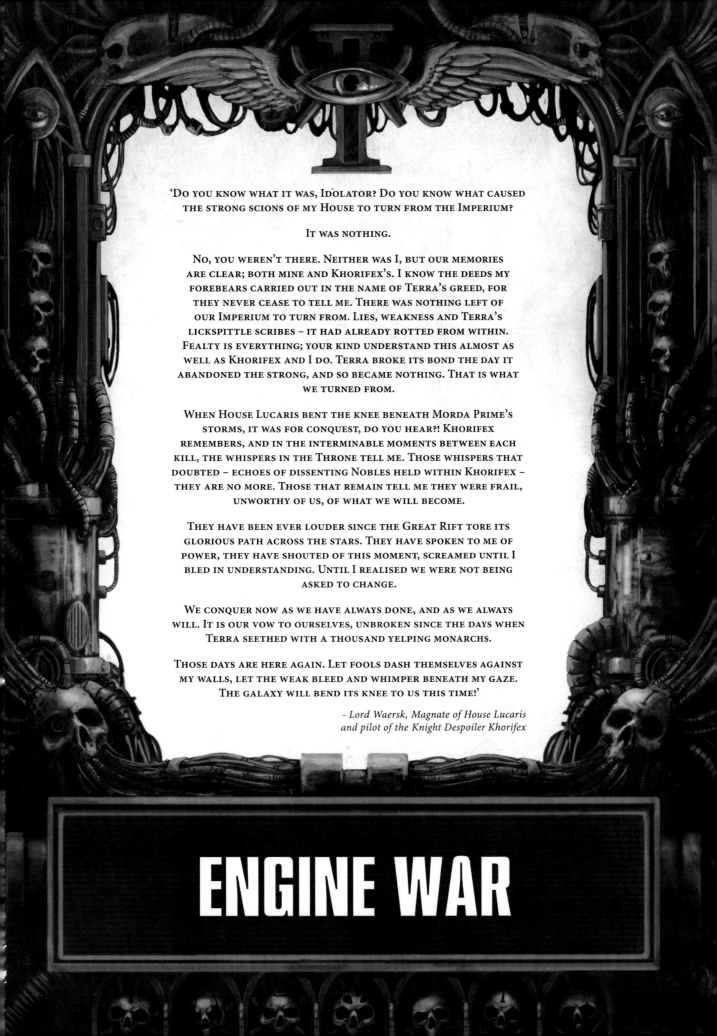

'Do you know what it was, Idolator? Do you know what caused the strong scions of my House to turn from the Imperium?

It was nothing.

No, you weren't there. Neither was I, but our memories are clear; both mine and Khorifex's. I know the deeds my forebears carried out in the name of Terra's greed, for they never cease to tell me. There was nothing left of our Imperium to turn from. Lies, weakness and Terra's lickspittle scribes – it had already rotted from within. Fealty is everything; your kind understand this almost as well as Khorifex and I do. Terra broke its bond the day it abandoned the strong, and so became nothing. That is what we turned from.

When House Lucaris bent the knee beneath Morda Prime's storms, it was for conquest, do you hear?! Khorifex remembers, and in the interminable moments between each kill, the whispers in the Throne tell me. Those whispers that doubted – echoes of dissenting Nobles held within Khorifex – they are no more. Those that remain tell me they were frail, unworthy of us, of what we will become.

They have been ever louder since the Great Rift tore its glorious path across the stars. They have spoken to me of power, they have shouted of this moment, screamed until I bled in understanding. Until I realised we were not being asked to change.

We conquer now as we have always done, and as we always will. It is our vow to ourselves, unbroken since the days when Terra seethed with a thousand yelping monarchs.

Those days are here again. Let fools dash themselves against my walls, let the weak bleed and whimper beneath my gaze. The galaxy will bend its knee to us this time!'

- Lord Waersk, Magnate of House Lucaris
and pilot of the Knight Despoiler Khorifex

ENGINE WAR

CONTENTS

PRODUCED BY THE WARHAMMER STUDIO

With thanks to the Mournival and the Infinity Circuit for their additional playtesting services

INTRODUCTION

Twisted by savage psychic storms in the aftermath of the Great Rift's emergence, the galaxy has become a darker place. Its sectors and systems are more isolated, and fell designs are able to coalesce in neglected regions. On the nightmarish industrial world of Ordex-Thaag, a confluence of prideful ambition leads to war.

The vast forces of the Imperium cannot be everywhere. Even coordinated and commanded by the champions of Humanity and made up of billions of courageous warriors, the Imperium's fleets and armies are stretched to breaking point. The number of systems left to fend for themselves – forgotten, abandoned or simply unreachable – grows daily. Within such environs, the Imperium's enemies grow strong, and even its allies feel the constraints of their oaths loosen.

The smog-shrouded planet of Ordex-Thaag is one such hidden blight; a fallen forge world, severed from Martian scrutiny and now stalked by Chaos Knights. The corrupted forges of this forgotten outpost of the Machine God are fuelled by the psychic emanations of techno-sorcery. The titanically cruel engines of the Chaos Knights and the Fallen Nobles who pilot them aim to use this malefic power to gouge another empyric rift through the Imperium. Others have witnessed the warp's taint spilling from the Cicatrix Maledictum. The Adeptus Mechanicus despair of its illogical and corrupting influence, and a sub-cult of renegade Tech-Priests seek to test a horrifying technology on Ordex-Thaag. The august Imperial Knights, meanwhile, are drawn to the planet by prophecy, yet revile the foul sorcery the warp begets. Both are willing to go to any lengths to push back the growing psychic tide.

Conceits and manias are converging on Ordex-Thaag, risking damnation in numbers enough to draw the attention of the Chaos Gods' daemonic servants. Opportunity exists, so the Daemons promise, for those with the will to act.

IN THIS BOOK

This book is part of Psychic Awakening, an ongoing series set in the aftermath of the Great Rift. It contains an overview from the perspectives of the Adeptus Mechanicus, the Imperial Knights, the Chaos Knights and the Chaos Daemons.

Inside you will find:

- The unfolding tale of the war on Ordex-Thaag; a vicious clash of obsession and hubris.

- A Theatre of War and missions to echo the Engine War storyline.

- Additional content for the four factions involved, including Stratagems, name generators, datasheets, updated points values, customisable forge world and Knight household army rules, and a great deal more.

THE TIDE OF POWER

When the Great Rift first split the galaxy and fractured the Imperium, few could have foreseen that beyond the initial devastation a flood of psychic power would flow from it. From every warp storm, the immaterium's corrupting influence seeped out, tainting everything with malignancy and challenging the supremacy of logic.

On Mars, the Adeptus Mechanicus felt its influence waning. It feared the loss of valuable resources and holy technologies. Most of all, it feared the risk of secession; of outposts whose loyalty to the Red Planet was already tenuous using isolation as a pretext to declare independence. To stave off such heresy, Mars reassigned many of its Explorator expeditions as Reclamation Fleets. They would re-contact the Adeptus Mechanicus' worlds, reminding them – by force if necessary – of their duty to Mars. Many forge worlds sent out fleets of their own, but none could match those of Mars in size or scope.

Magos Xu Kroll departed Mars in command of one of its three Reclamation Fleets, destined for the Segmentum Tempestus. The fleet made slow progress, buffeted by warp storms from one forge world to the next, with every ship suffering losses to its astropathic choir and bonded Navigators. Mars maintained trans-generational contracts with the finest Navigator Houses in the Imperium, yet here were their scions – as Kroll's closest advisers ranted to the other Magi around him – failing to guide the Omnissiah's servants from one divine node of his realm to another.

Kroll's fleet made contact with many worlds that owed direct fealty to Mars or declared an affiliation with the Red Planet. In every sector and system, on relay stations and in sunken forge temples, the Tech-Priest Dominus and his fleet's Magi beheld the Great Rift's continuing psychic corruption. On the mining world of Goborra, data-Daemons infected the servitor clades, twisting them into abominations that tore apart their masters. In the Archisanctorum, curators were consumed by a scrapcode entity, their possessed mechadendrites overloading the auto-chapel's reactor core, destroying the technological relics. On Darios, sentient warp sores bloomed within the Omnissiah's faithful, frail flesh and divine bionics running together like wax.

Many of the fleet's Magi could not process what they witnessed. Blinded by the loss of irreplaceable artefacts, some mentally discarded the illogical psychic occurrences, proclaiming their impossibility even as they unfolded before their optics. Tech-Priests went insane trying to categorise the unnatural power they saw manifested by indentured sump-scum declared 'machine-touched'; by previously sanctioned psykers who now vomited black fire; or by polymorphic Daemons crawling from warp tears.

The Adeptus Mechanicus' interests – Mars' interests – were suffering, and dogma demanded a reaction. Stoked by the anti-psychic rhetoric that the likes of Dominus Kroll and his circling advisers espoused, the Reclamation Fleets expended the resources of entire systems as they sought to preserve the Adeptus Mechanicus' power. Ancient technologies were deployed and field testing of unstable weapons was expanded. The greatest minds of Mars sought to turn back the flood of psychic aberration using every esoteric force and every ally they possessed.

So vital was the future of the forge worlds that few of the Reclamation Fleets quested alone. Many were accompanied by troop transports of the Astra Militarum, orbital assault vessels of the Adepta Sororitas and war barges of knightly households carrying their Nobles and towering suits. Like the fleets of Mars, many Great Houses of Imperial Knights strove to extinguish the corruption pouring from the Great Rift. Few did so more fervently than the Knights of the Padah March, which joined Kroll's Reclamation Fleet as it entered the Segmentum Tempestus.

The Padah March was a heraldic alliance of Nobles from many systems. At their head was Baroness Sordhen of House Terryn, who nursed a hatred of sorcery and witchcraft and yet surrounded herself with a coterie of soothsayers, hierophants and readers of the Emperor's Tarot. Many of the Nobles who followed Sordhen bore scars dealt by rogue psykers and pyroclastic cults. Their monastic Sacristans had restored melted shields and twisted armour, but many Freeblades also carried recently applied memorials; dark reminders of entire lances of their kin brought low by malefic power.

Wherever they turned, the Reclamation Fleets encountered nihilistic slaughter and the blasphemous defilement of the Machine God's manifest divinity.

Nowhere was this more sickening than in the tainted forms of Chaos Knights. Dread lances of these unhallowed relics emerged from the maws of warp storms to conquer and enslave in greater numbers than before. Systems whose communications had been crippled by the Great Rift were preyed upon by the cruel and monstrous engines, even as calamitous empyric manifestations embroiled their defences.

With warp storms continuing to dog their endeavours, Kroll's Reclamation Fleet unearthed pict-captures on the devastated industrial world of Sturmveil. The images showed city-continents strewn with death. Malice-filled Chaos Knights could be seen breaking apart the warded fortifications holding the planet's psyker-tithe. While the world burned around them, the war machines herded throngs of witches, cult demagogues and miracle-makers into foetid mass conveyers. Many of these Chaos Knights bore the serpentine badge of House Lucaris, but numerous other households were present; oath-breakers both recognised and unknown.

Suddenly, the warp storms intensified. As Kroll and his advisers turned from the pict-captures, the entire fleet was swallowed in a tempest of power. Some ships broke apart, while others simply vanished. On the brink of annihilation, a faint signal broke through – in desperation, Kroll followed it.

'The Angulum *is gone, Dominus Kroll. Its signal has simply ceased, I cannot–*'

'Dominus Kroll, request from Baroness Sordhen, she–'

'Cease! Third-tier choir intercepting extrinsic signal, Imperial choriform signature.'

'We cannot be sure of its provenance, Dominus; the signal bears an unusual Morus pentameter.'

'We do not serve Mars if we are inoperable. Alert the rest of the fleet at once. Instruct Navigator Prose; the signal's source is our destination.'

MUNDUS MALEFICA

Circled by a spiral of empyric force, the world of Ordex-Thaag has remained hidden from Mars since its fall centuries ago. The once-loyal forge world now serves a hellish pack of Chaos Knights, while deep within the planet, fell technology tears the void apart.

Experimental data-cell ZV3, continuous passive recording maintained. Psysonorum appl. echo-capture>>\
Location: Forge Senioris, Ordex-Thaag…

This is the eleventh shipment of these witches we have delivered to you, and what progress is there? Be very careful, priest. Remember that you and your tainted cabal are here upon my sufferance. Your access to this forge world's shrines and data-stacks is within my gift – as are your lives.

Do not deceive yourselves into thinking me blind. My household Idolators keep me appraised of every movement made by you and your… creations.

You have a promise to keep. Tear this segmentum apart, and you will have whatever you want. As long as the serfs of Terra witness how great our reach has become, I don't care if a thousand worlds burn.

The Imperium will bow before House Lucaris and all will fear the name of Magnate Waersk!

+++END DATA-TRACT+++

A minor forge world of the Soelich Sub-sector, Ordex-Thaag was finally abandoned in 633.M41 when greenskins proved unstoppable in their rapacious trawl for resources and slaves. The Orks eventually moved on, but the servants of the Machine God could not spare the assets required to re-establish their presence on the planet, as attacks by other xenos and the Great Enemy had intensified elsewhere over the decades.

So far as the Tech-Priests knew, the Ordex System lay in ruin, its forges cold and its temples untended. Mars heard occasional rumours from Soelich void-riggers of ever increasing numbers of razed worlds in the sector, but these ceased when the Great Rift tore its way across the galaxy and the immense warp anomaly of the Siren's Storm ruptured into existence. Had the Adeptus Mechanicus known what truly transpired upon Ordex-Thaag and understood the nature of the Siren's Storm, nothing would have held back the Machine God's wrath.

In truth, the Ordex System had fallen under the heel of Chaos Knights and a cabal of Daemon-splicers from the Dark Mechanicum; traitor Tech-Priests who were a dark mirror to the Adeptus Mechanicus. Driven by their desire for the techno-arcana jealously sequestered by the Adeptus Mechanicus, the Daemon-splicers had approached Magnate Waersk, a Fallen Noble of House Lucaris fuelled by hatred for Terra and an obsession to see his household raised to its rightful place of dominance. If the claims they made to Waersk held true, such artefacts would soon be within his gift to bestow. Waersk did not know if the fallen Tech-Priests could be trusted, and he laid layers of contingency in place for their termination. Yet if even half their claims manifested, House Lucaris would hold immense power in its gauntlet. Fear would swell and ripen in the Imperium, and the Fanged Knights of House Lucaris could wield fear better than any.

On Ordex-Thaag, the hereteks used warp-fuelled Daemon Engines to drill their way straight through the planet's core. At its heart they installed corrupted machines, binding daemonic essences to them with agonising runic chains and fuelling their torture with the sacrifices of psykers delivered in their hundreds by the Chaos Knights. Along thousands of miles of shielded channels, their octagonal lengths inscribed with foul runes, the Daemons' hatred and pain twisted and pulsed.

The eldritch power that was generated acted like a hook on the veil separating the warp from the material realm. As Ordex-Thaag rotated and orbited its parent star, the spindle of soul-stuff span and tightened. Its effects reached out into the immaterium, pulling on the tempest of the Siren's Storm and forcing the breach to rupture further and further. There were worlds in its path: fortress worlds, planetary munitions silos and orbital docking facilities; billions of lives and some of the Imperium's greatest southern defences. Yet these were merely collateral damage compared to the true target. The black-hearted techno-sorcerers claimed they could twist the warp rift around the Ordex System before sending it inexorably towards Terra and the Golden Throne.

Ordex-Thaag was now a world of tainted industry and feudal horror. Beneath the ruined forge temples of the Adeptus Mechanicus, their dark kin's manufactorums and blasphemous ritual sites were buried deep, like poisonous barbs in the planet's crust. Miles-long fissures scarred the blasted landscape, city-sized macro-vents along their perimeters belching a vile smog thick with psychic effluvia. Shards of predatory sentience, clouds of corrosive vapour and spreading pools of toxic witchfire befouled the planet's surface.

Above the Daemon-splicers' domain, the towering keeps and fortifications of Waersk and the Fallen Nobles who attended his court stood proud of the desolation. Waersk had drawn to his banner not only Lucaris Knights, but also roving Dreadblades; bitter warriors bereft of even the honour of a Household. By far the greatest of the citadels was the Qysberg, a series of ringed fortifications dozens of miles across. Built through the artifice of Waersk's Idolators and by the back-breaking labour of enslaved warriors, its labyrinthine ways hid all manner of mechanised traps.

The Qysberg's central keep guarded one end of the titanic borehole that ran straight through the planet, its battlements bristling with weapon emplacements and profane icons. On the other side of the world, the cowled Daemon-splicers had raised an enormous pyramidal resonator-spire that magnified the trapped Daemons' psychic howls of rage. Stolen Imperial technology, monolithic in size and dating back millennia, had been subverted and grafted into a morass of blood-caked antennae, emitters and fleshy protuberances, and a congeries of sentience throbbed throughout it.

It was the leaking emotions from this resonator-spire, entwined with ancient Imperial signal forms, which Dominus Kroll's Reclamation Fleet had intercepted. Four of his third-tier Astropaths had died in agony at its touch, but their sacrifice leached away the daemonic taint. What remained was undeniably Imperial in origin, but saturated with hues, tastes and sensations that were ancient and unsettling.

The other Tech-Priests who thronged the flagship's bridge had blurted concerns about the signal, but only Kroll had received the Astropaths' full analysis. The Tech-Priest Dominus knew exactly what the signal represented, and disclosed this knowledge to his trusted advisers who shared his wider ambitions. Whatever was on Ordex-Thaag was saturated in psychic power.

At the thought, a recurrent loop of hate arose once more in Kroll's subroutines; unsolvable, illogical, changeable… *vile*. There would be casualties. His plan would imperil the ancient and holy Knight suits. But the Omnissiah was with him, he told himself. The Omnissiah and the Varlian Device.

TECH-FLEETS of RECLAMATION

Ref Rbx 1010011010
Projected course of
known Reclamation
Fleets produced under
the Fabricator Locum of
Holy Mars. Dat: error.

SEGMENTUM OBSCURUS

HALO STARS

SCARUS SECTOR

FINIAL SECTOR

CALIXIS SECTOR

Lathe Worlds

The Eye of Terror

Daxos Gemini

Lucius

3

GOTHIC SECTOR

STORM OF THE EMPEROR'S WRATH

Mordian

VALHALLA

MATARAKH

Nachmund Gauntlet

Alaric Prime

KRASTELLAN

IMPERIUM

Cadia

Agripinaa

Molech

CICATRIX MALEDICTUM

Armageddon

Elysia

Voss Prime

SEGMENTUM SOLAR

Ryza

Sarum

The Maelstrom

Stygies

2

Chrysis

Mars

Catachan

Badab

SEGMENTUM PACIFICUS

Estaban System

Krieg

UHULIS SECTOR

Tallarn

4

Siren's Storm

1

Graia

Xendu

Kimdaria

Metalica

SEGMENTUM TEMPESTUS

5

Morda Prime

Gryphonne IV

Raisa

REDUCTUS SECTOR

Rapture

Jedathra

THE VEILED REGION

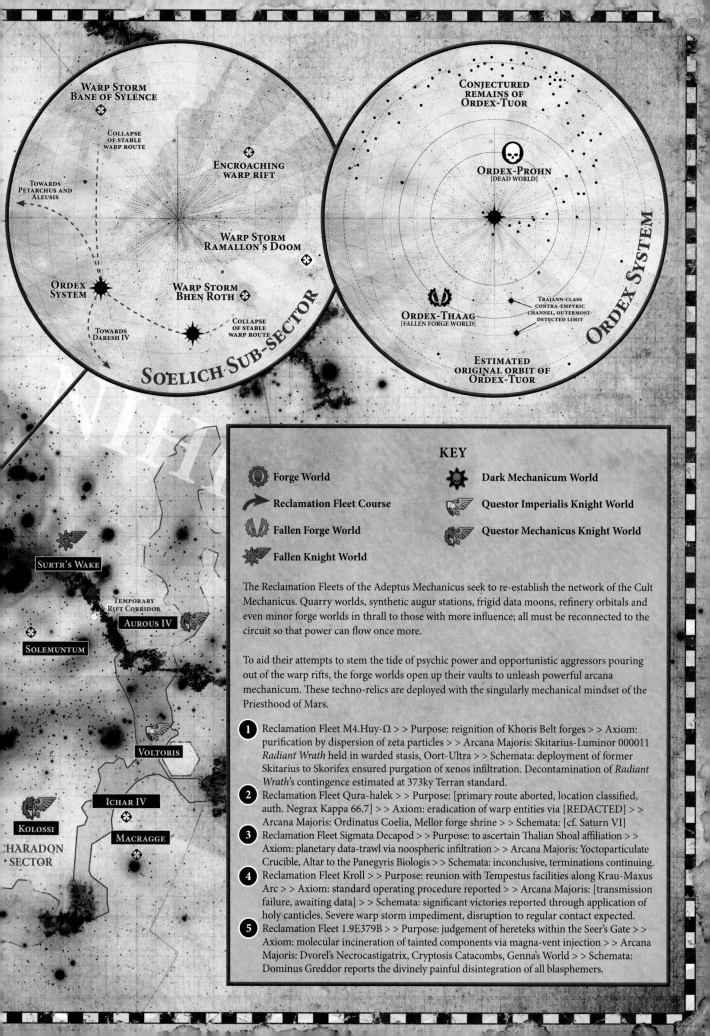

SOELICH SUB-SECTOR

WARP STORM
BANE OF SYLENCE

COLLAPSE
OF STABLE
WARP ROUTE

ENCROACHING
WARP RIFT

TOWARDS
PETARCHUS AND
ALEUSIS

WARP STORM
RAMALLON'S DOOM

ORDEX
SYSTEM

WARP STORM
BHEN ROTH

TOWARDS
DARESH IV

COLLAPSE
OF STABLE
WARP ROUTE

ORDEX SYSTEM

CONJECTURED
REMAINS OF
ORDEX-TUOR

ORDEX-PROHN
[DEAD WORLD]

ORDEX-THAAG
[FALLEN FORGE WORLD]

TRAJANN-CLASS
CONTRA-EMPYRIC
CHANNEL, OUTERMOST-
DETECTED LIMIT

ESTIMATED
ORIGINAL ORBIT OF
ORDEX-TUOR

RIFT

SURTR'S WAKE

TEMPORARY
RIFT CORRIDOR

AUROUS IV

SOLEMUNTUM

VOLTORIS

ICHAR IV

KOLOSSI

MACRAGGE

CHARADON
SECTOR

KEY

Forge World

Dark Mechanicum World

Reclamation Fleet Course

Questor Imperialis Knight World

Fallen Forge World

Questor Mechanicus Knight World

Fallen Knight World

The Reclamation Fleets of the Adeptus Mechanicus seek to re-establish the network of the Cult Mechanicus. Quarry worlds, synthetic augur stations, frigid data moons, refinery orbitals and even minor forge worlds in thrall to those with more influence; all must be reconnected to the circuit so that power can flow once more.

To aid their attempts to stem the tide of psychic power and opportunistic aggressors pouring out of the warp rifts, the forge worlds open up their vaults to unleash powerful arcana mechanicum. These techno-relics are deployed with the singularly mechanical mindset of the Priesthood of Mars.

1 Reclamation Fleet M4.Huy-Ω > > Purpose: reignition of Khoris Belt forges > > Axiom: purification by dispersion of zeta particles > > Arcana Majoris: Skitarius-Luminor 000011 *Radiant Wrath* held in warded stasis, Oort-Ultra > > Schemata: deployment of former Skitarius to Skorifex ensured purgation of xenos infiltration. Decontamination of *Radiant Wrath*'s contingence estimated at 373ky Terran standard.

2 Reclamation Fleet Qura-halek > > Purpose: [primary route aborted, location classified, auth. Negrax Kappa 66.7] > > Axiom: eradication of warp entities via [REDACTED] > > Arcana Majoris: Ordinatus Coelia, Mellor forge shrine > > Schemata: [cf. Saturn VI]

3 Reclamation Fleet Sigmata Decapod > > Purpose: to ascertain Thalian Shoal affiliation > > Axiom: planetary data-trawl via noospheric infiltration > > Arcana Majoris: Yoctoparticulate Crucible, Altar to the Panegyris Biologis > > Schemata: inconclusive, terminations continuing.

4 Reclamation Fleet Kroll > > Purpose: reunion with Tempestus facilities along Krau-Maxus Arc > > Axiom: standard operating procedure reported > > Arcana Majoris: [transmission failure, awaiting data] > > Schemata: significant victories reported through application of holy canticles. Severe warp storm impediment, disruption to regular contact expected.

5 Reclamation Fleet 1.9E379B > > Purpose: judgement of hereteks within the Seer's Gate > > Axiom: molecular incineration of tainted components via magna-vent injection > > Arcana Majoris: Dvorel's Necrocastigatrix, Cryptosis Catacombs, Genna's World > > Schemata: Dominus Greddor reports the divinely painful disintegration of all blasphemers.

TECHNIS OBLIGATUS

Tech-Priest Dominus Kroll had finally manoeuvred his plans towards fruition, and was poised to unleash a terrible technology upon the warped foulness within the Qysberg.

Noospheric
permeation, theta-
binharic horometer.
<Regulus Prime,
Technaesthetist
Gorn Virellan>

Hail the Blessed Cog!

The blasphemies we have borne witness to will remain upon my mnemo-wafers until my expiration. On every subject world of Mars we reached, there was evidence of empyric anomaly, even though the probabilities of such occurrences are minute. We accessed pict-logs of unaugmented civilians extruding exothermic phenomena into servants of the Omnissiah. Elsewhere, hereteks had used holy power cores to vitalise annelid devices, their intent unknown.

It is so obvious now. Magos Kroll has explained all. The sensation of understanding approximates the endowment of a new augmentation, and I feel closer to the Machine God. So many variables, but Magos Kroll has shown their root, and holy clarity is the result.

If Mars will not act against the psyker flood, then we must.

++END TRANSMISSION++

As Kroll's Reclamation Fleet approached the source of the psychic signal, the Tech-Priest Dominus revealed his plans to his fellow Magi. Ordex-Thaag, he told them, was tainted by defilers of the Machine God's works. The Red Planet had an obligation to defend technology's primacy in the face of corruption.

But just as the galaxy was riven with warp storms, so was the Adeptus Mechanicus fractured at its core. Secretive sub-cults divided the Priesthood of Mars, each with their own interpretations of the Great Rift's aftermath. Kroll and his advisers belonged to the hidden sect known as the Teeth of the Cog, which abhorred every form of psychic power as a dire threat to the Adeptus Mechanicus. From Astropaths and Navigators to the battle-psykers of the Adeptus Astartes, none were above the cult's revulsion. They kept this absolutism secret, however; many on Mars jealously guarded the contracts of exotic fabrication they held with the Imperium's psychic institutions.

Thus Kroll chose his words carefully. Through means he did not divulge to the Magi, the Teeth of the Cog had acquired the Varlian Device – a complex detonator intended to suppress psychic effects with a powerful null-pulse. The device would be unleashed against the traitors, he explained, and its concept proved unambiguously. Its successful deployment would be a triumph of pure logic over ephemeral witchery. After all they had witnessed on the journey from Mars, the Magi's passionless detachment was overridden, replaced by binharic brays for war.

Even the lowest battlements of the Qysberg's black outer wall stood twice the height of a Knight suit. Even now, the superstitious Baroness Sordhen was leading many of her companions to the surface to strike at the citadel's southern gatehouse. Angular bastions jutted out, their crenellations thick with weapons arrays clinging to them like the nests of vast avian predators. Kroll authorised diversionary attacks on the walls to the north and south while he directed the major assault in the west.

The Martian cohorts attacked in carefully calculated waves; an algorithm of war that predicted an acceptable margin of victory. Ranks of Skitarii marched towards the Qysberg's outer wall, while lines of Skorpius Duneriders hovered in traditional patterns behind them. Maniples of battle servitors rolled or ambled forward under every conceivable form of locomotion, auto-loaders spooling.

As the opening canticle of praise spread amid the faithful, packs of Onager engines fired neutron lasers. The strikes impacted on the Qysberg's flanks, each blinding beam detonating in a blast of disruptive energy. Kroll brought ever more esoteric weapons to bear. Crackling lances of power and arcing spheres of energy battered the defences until they cracked. Sizzling spheres of phosphor found their way into the ruptures, causing the very rockcrete to ignite.

The Qysberg itself had responded violently the instant Kroll's forces were within range. Multiple heavy weapon mounts located under the battlements fired streams of solid shot, explosive shells and searing laser fire. Servitors and Skitarii exploded in showers of bloody components or fell with fist-sized holes burned through their bodies.

Maniples of Kastelan Robots advanced to the wall's foot, before single-mindedly ramming their fists into it, mechanically tearing the defences apart piece by piece until a section of wall finally crumbled. Kroll pushed his warriors swiftly through the breach, the Varlian Device borne before him on a floating bier shielded by conversion fields. Ironstrider engines picked their way through while Archaeopter Fusilaves glided overhead, unleashing payloads of seismic munitions that undermined walls and disrupted defences.

Now the Chaos Knights unleashed their ire, and the invaders discovered the citadel's true potential. With every courtyard the disciples of the Machine God breached, the traitors and their fortress tore more of the attackers apart. The deeper Kroll's forces

pushed, the higher the curtain walls became, smothering them in a deepening twilight. From titanic embrasures, Chaos Knights shot rapid-firing battle cannons, laser destructors and volcano lances, scything apart mechanised frames faster than sanctified auto-simulacra could repair them.

Sections of the curtain walls ground apart or closed together to the clanking of hidden cogs, exposing the Martian forces or cutting them off from each other. From the battlements, fierce gargoyles and immense heraldic beast-forms vomited caustic fire, or came alive to sweep warriors over causeways with clawed limbs of stone.

From hidden postern gates, more Chaos Knights lunged, crushing knots of Skitarii underfoot before unleashing titanic salvoes of firepower on the move. Some loosed flurries of explosive missiles and rockets at point-blank range, seemingly relishing the backwash of fire and carnage that flowed over them.

In an outer courtyard, a huge iron grid was lifted from the ground by thick chains, and from within the fortress' bowels burst a rabid and visceral Knight. As its steps quickened, saw-blades set in the soles of its feet whined and sparked. Carbine slugs from Skitarii Vanguard burned up in the giant machine's red-tinged ion shield, while heavier fire from Skorpius Disintegrators only fuelled its berserk onslaught. Combat walkers and battle tanks were crushed and torn, and dozens of Mars' warriors were shredded in fountains of bloody oil.

Dominus Kroll became desperate. His isolated forces were being picked apart, and scattered victories could not be capitalised on. Time had run out to get the Varlian Device to the prime location. With his most capable Battle Maniple, Kroll fought his way back to the outer wall breach, leaving the device guarded by his remaining servitors. Canting a final prayer, he sent a remote signal and the device activated.

THE VARLIAN DEVICE

Not even Dominus Kroll was certain of where the artefact known as the Varlian Device had come from. Nor would he ever admit that he did not fully understand its function or effects.

The Teeth of the Cog had been approached by an unknown Tech-Priest. How this nameless Magos had divined the sub-cult's existence was disturbing, but he spoke of bonds of shared knowledge with those he represented. He divulged no noospheric data, however, claiming through a vox-emitter that he protected the identity of his masters. Minute, insectile servitors scurried amongst his robes as he congratulated the Teeth of the Cog for their insight into the corruptive influence of psychic power and the need to stamp it out for the good of the Imperium and the galaxy.

The secretive Magos told of how an Explorator Fleet in his forge world's sector had uncovered the ancient core of an STC for a defensive mechanism.

His masters had unravelled its secrets and built the device, but they needed a suitable testing ground and like-minded devotees to the Imperium's future.

As large as a battle servitor, the device's housing lay on an anti-grav bier. The shadowy Tech-Priest explained how it could extinguish the taint of sorcery, releasing a pulse of null-energy to throw off the warp's grasping hold on human minds. Thus the monstrous denizens of the immaterium would be banished forever, and the Adeptus Mechanicus would be feted for saving the Imperium.

When the Teeth of the Cog pressed their guest on the origin of the device, he gave a static-laced bark of laughter and said it might as well have come from the Gates of Varl. Quarantined for millennia, that haunted region had become a byword for ineffable knowledge and undefinable constants. But the Teeth of the Cog were too awestruck by the offered device to denounce this impropriety.

BEACON OF CORRUPTION

Seeking to silence the unholy resonator-spire, Imperial Knights of the Padah March vowed to rip its foul root out of Ordex-Thaag's crust. The servants of the Dark Gods were loathe to see Magnate Waersk's endeavour cut short, however, and strained the veil shielding realspace in their hunger to tear the Imperial Knights down.

Taking his first stride upon the surface of Ordex-Thaag, Sir Dhekar of House Terryn felt the rumble of underground tremors through Drakefyre's limbs. The honoured Knight Errant responded smoothly to Sir Dhekar's control as they joined the other Knights of the Burning Spear; the lance formed to topple the resonator-spire. Sir Dhekar had pledged to Baroness Sordhen that he would see that structure burned to ash, and never had he failed to keep a vow.

The resonator-spire was the source of the signal the Reclamation Fleet had followed in its desperation to escape the warp storms, and Kroll had informed Sordhen that it mirrored the position of the traitor fastness in Ordex-Thaag's northern hemisphere. While the Baroness led the majority of the Padah March to tear open the black citadel of the Qysberg, she was determined to ensure that whatever fell power dwelt there could not somehow survive on the planet's far side.

Sordhen had shared the visions of her seers with her Nobles. She had interpreted their tales of a two-headed serpent as a reference to the twin evils of the Qysberg and the resonator-spire, and requested her Nobles to forgo fighting alongside her in order to secure the spire's destruction. Sir Dhekar, Lady Olwyn and Sir Geherys proclaimed their acceptance of the quest, alongside young Nobles piloting Armigers and the Freeblade Sir Morghant of Torres III.

It was Sir Geherys who first laid eyes on the construct. An obelisk festooned with branching brass aerials and snaking conduits, it stood half as tall again as his Knight Valiant, Felbane. Cuneiform markings were intricately incised into its surfaces, and amongst the mass of spars and cables, lengths of fleshy tumours pulsed. Steaming blood matted its surface and pooled at the base, staining it in browns and reds, while a buzzing cloud of flies surrounded it.

Omnipresent earthquakes ground through the fractured terrain. Chasms, cracks and fumaroles radiated outwards from the resonator-spire. Their sides were encrusted with foul growths, and from within came the putrid emanations of the Dark Mechanicum's hidden forges, tainted with psychic run-off. Discarded mistakes – or escapees – crawled in the depths of each opening, or haunted them as splintered shades stripped down to predatory sentiences. Sickly-coloured fumes twisted into shapes suggestive of fanged maws, while streams of toxic fluids burned and warped anything they touched. With each fissure the Knights passed, metallic growls and wafts of scrambled code littered their vox-net.

Before the Burning Spear reached the resonator-spire, Lady Olwyn and her aggressive Knight Paladin, Honour Adamantus, alerted the lance to a patch of sky above their target's pinnacle. A bulge of sickly light swam there, spinning and darkening. Then the air all around the construct swiftly condensed into a vapour the colour of bile, with shadows moving within it.

Reacting to the Knights' proximity, the shadows in the mist pulled themselves from its embrace, their diffuse forms cohering into clawed and horned Daemons. The ground shook as the fissures surrounding the resonator-spire appeared to roar in welcome, belching dark fumes and multicoloured flames.

The Nobles of the Burning Spear beheld the creatures in horror and outrage. Never had they faced such unholy evil. Memories surfaced of terrors struck down by saints in Imperial scripture. Warnings bled into their minds from the imprinted spirits within their Thrones Mechanicum, as former pilots relived the hunts of Old Night. The Nobles realised the vile depths to which Ordex-Thaag's masters had sunk, and hatred filled them. Sir Dhekar led them in the Lay of the Hunt and ordered the hell-spawn destroyed.

The Knights unleashed a thunderous opening salvo. Dozens of Daemons disappeared in the conflagration, and many more were ripped to pieces that dissipated in sulphurous wisps. With Sir Dhekar and Lady Olwyn at their fore, the Knights strode straight towards the resonator-spire.

More Daemons eagerly forced their way through the breach around the spire, and warp-spawned hosts also manifested to the Knights' flanks. Sir Morghant urged the

lance forward as his Knight Paladin Scion of Torres became wreathed in a corposant of witchfire and a diseased mass of Plaguebearers tore at his armour. Layers of hyper-dense alloy blistered and corroded beneath the Daemons' corrupting blades, and the Knight was soon lost to the others, the fumes swallowing him as the roar of his weapons receded.

Nearing the spire, Drakefyre raised its thermal cannon and fired, but the sudden jolt of an enormous earth tremor saw its superheated beam go wide. Streaking missiles from Felbane hit the obelisk, tearing chunks from it and raising howls from the Daemons. Sir Geherys cheered as he saw the bulging patch of sky dim, some Daemons denaturing. Yet the Knights were not causing enough damage, and they were being surrounded. Sir Dhekar bade those around him to hold the Daemons back and carve a route for him as he made for the spire, but regardless of how many they felled, their company continued to shrink.

From the chasms clambered mechanical horrors possessed with daemonic hunger. With a huge iron claw, one grabbed for an Armiger Helverin whose autocannons were tearing apart a sweep of Burning Chariots. The young Noble's Knight fell and was dragged, kicking, down into the pit.

Honour Adamantus was charged by a towering winged beast, its fur dripping with blood. Deflecting

axe strikes of enormous strength, Lady Olwyn duelled savagely with the Bloodthirster. A scything blow ripped open her chassis, missing her mortal frame by inches, but in return she plunged her reaper chainsword into the monster and drove the weapon up into its head. The shout of victory from her ichor-sprayed Throne was short-lived, as Furies dove into the Knight's open chassis and tore Lady Olwyn apart. Felbane, meanwhile, was surrounded, its cannons switching from target to target to keep the encroaching horrors at bay.

Drakefyre reached the resonator-spire just as a lithe apparition stalked from behind it. A blindingly fast whip of sinew struck out, only just stopped by Drakefyre's ion shield before a long blade and dread claws precisely carved into linkages and drive systems. Drakefyre's thermal cannon hung limply as Sir Dhekar sought in vain to land a telling blow on his tormentor.

From the fumes it had vanished into, the colossal metal form of Scion of Torres suddenly charged. It was barely recognisable, shedding flaking and melted armour with every step. The Daemon assailing Drakefyre was quick enough to turn and strike, burying its claw in the Freeblade Knight's carapace and impaling Sir Morghant, but it could not withdraw the limb in time. The crippled Knight crashed into the Daemon and bore it to the ground, pinning the creature down.

Sir Morghant's sacrifice had bought Drakefyre a reprieve. Drive systems protesting, Sir Dhekar drove the Knight Errant's thunderstrike gauntlet into the resonator-spire and tore out whatever bloody devices powered it. The bulging warp sore above the spire imploded, and an aftershock whipped across the battlefield, ripping the Daemons out of existence. A sheet of energy flashed heavenward, and the spire collapsed in a clamour of screaming metal and tearing flesh.

HONOUR AND OBSESSION

While Dominus Kroll attacked the Qysberg at several points, Baroness Sordhen led the Knights of the Padah March in a frontal attack on its gatehouse. Her increasingly voluble seers had seen portents of witchcraft and the covenants of the damned. The gallantry of House Terryn would, she vowed, see the Chaos Knights destroyed.

From orbit, Baroness Sordhen of House Terryn had likened the Qysberg to a swelling infection, seeing it rendered in the glow of a holo-projection. The ships of the Padah March had survived the ferocious warp storms around Ordex-Thaag, and maintained a wide orbit of the planet away from the ships of Dominus Kroll's Reclamation Fleet.

The Tech-Priest had provided the information Sordhen had desperately sought – confirmation of her seers' prophecies. Their readings of the Emperor's Tarot had repeatedly dealt the Spyndle, upon which crouches the witch, tormenting the fates of the righteous. Kroll confirmed that the signal his fleet had received was indeed befouled with warp-craft.

Sordhen's attack on the Qysberg was brutally direct, but carefully planned. As well as the lance she had sent south to tear down the resonator-spire, the Baroness dispatched three further lances of proud Nobles to bastions that surrounded her point of attack. In this way, she aimed to ensure that no traitors could attack their forces from the rear.

For her main thrust, Baroness Sordhen led a cavalcade of three lances straight towards the Qysberg's primary armoured gatehouse, a mile from where Dominus Kroll's forces attacked the walls. Twenty four other Knights of all classes strode with their liege. More than half were scions of House Terryn, but the Houses of Oebbern, Griffith and Firehame all flew the pennants of their distant kin with pride.

Ensconced upon the Throne Mechanicum of the Knight Warden Bright Destroyer, Baroness Sordhen led all three lances in a closely packed wedge. Already, defensive fire was reaching them, glancing from pauldrons and ion shields.

Knights with longer-ranged guns moved at the fore and flanks, and their weapons roared in response. Battle cannon shells and stormspear rockets streaked towards the battlements, while siegebreaker cannons pummelled the bastion's energy shields. Armiger Helverins targeted the Qysberg's weapon sconces, blinding their sensors with squalls of interference. Shielded in the formation's midst stomped Knights Valiant and Gallant; close-ranged brawlers that no fortress walls can withstand once they have been reached.

Coordinating their ion shields in defence, the Knights advanced up the gatehouse's inclined avenue, past grisly trophies. When those on the edges of the formation suffered damage they moved back, their place taken by another as the firepower pouring down on them increased with every step they took.

The gatehouse's shields finally overloaded from the Imperial Knights' relentless attacks, and expired in a sheet of ejected flame.

Now, Knight Castellans moved to the fore. Ancient weapons sent out the burning heat of stars, and eruptions of fire and liquid rock burst from the wall. The formation reached the gatehouse, whose black walls rose to three times the Knights' height, and a trio of Knights Valiant sent their thundercoil harpoons slamming into its cyclopean masonry. The power fed along their chains fried the gatehouse's remaining defences. Then the weapons were winched back in, anchored by the weight of the Knights wielding them, and the colossal walls crumbled and fell.

The breach was made, and Knights from the formation's centre charged through it, smashing aside any remaining obstacles with thunderous blows from their huge gauntlets.

Three Knights perished as they fought their way through the gatehouse's cathedra-sized interior. Streams of caustic chemicals poured from murder holes, metal spars shot from hidden gravitic rails and prehensile technovirus injectors coiled from the shadows. The Qysberg's maze of courtyards constantly changed to the clank and grind of hidden machinery. When the Padah March emerged into the first of them, the citadel's true scale hit Baroness Sordhen, but she could not stop now.

At that moment the Chaos Knights fell upon the invaders in surges of ground-shaking hatred. Dozens of warped engines, their malformed carapaces thick with spines and leering faces, emerged from hidden transit-ways or attacked from rotating embrasures.

The planet's tectonic activity was drowned out by the shuddering impacts of tons of metal crashing into each other, roars from emitter grilles and the blasts of immense weaponry. Reaper chainswords sheared off weapon mounts as gauntlets smashed and tore through armoured cowlings. At close range the traitors' greater numbers began to tell, as did the superior mobility afforded them by the Qysberg's hidden ways.

Baroness Sordhen lashed out in frustration and rising despair, but she could not ignore the mounting losses. She yearned to take as many enemies with her as possible, yet she was responsible for her fellow Knights. Filled with anger, she called the retreat. As the Padah March began to withdraw to their initial breach, Sordhen vainly tried to raise Dominus Kroll by vox.

Chaos Knights hounded them, crippling with gatling cannons and laser destructors, pulling down any who were too slow. To the west, Sordhen saw the remnants of the Adeptus Mechanicus streaming back across the cracked plain, their own battle clearly lost as well.

Suddenly, an explosion erupted from where the Omnissiah's servants had been fighting. An expanding shell of energy enveloped the Qysberg and raced towards all three forces. The null-field caught the retreating Skitarii and servitors first. Many slowed and then simply stopped, arms limp, but those clustered around data-tethers appeared to fare better. The Knights of both sides suffered more grievously. Within their Thrones Mechanicum, imprinted gheists screamed as they were stripped away, the feedback slaying their

Nobles. Several Knights collapsed, their pilots' souls engulfed in cascades of entropy.

Almost as quickly as it had struck, the null-field dissipated, and the remaining Imperial Knights managed to outpace their reeling pursuers. Sordhen praised the Emperor that the Padah March had weathered the explosion better than the traitors, though she could not explain how. Intercepting Dominus Kroll to demand answers, she found the Tech-Priest rambling about a device… his triumph… acceptable losses. At first Sordhen thought Kroll afflicted, but then realised the deaths of her companions had been his doing. Her gauntlet snatched him up, crushing the mass of bionic limbs beneath his torso. As she bore him back to the Knights' landing barges, she ignored his screams and the paltry fire of his Skitarii.

DAEMONSURGE

As Sordhen returned to her ship, the daemonic essences bound within Ordex-Thaag's core felt the effects of the Varlian Device – its prematurely activated null-field had disrupted the shackles that tormented them. Fuelled by thoughts of vengeance and bloodlust, they broke free, surging to the surface with an almighty roar.

The effects of the Varlian Device had penetrated Ordex-Thaag's surface and shattered the wards binding the daemonic essences within the planet's core. Centuries of torment were visited back upon the Daemon-splicers a thousandfold, as four surviving entities ripped apart the hereteks and their dreadful machinery.

Yet there was one these exalted Daemons loathed above all others; he who had presided over their prison – Magnate Waersk. As vortices of energy, the four warp-spawned essences tore their way to the surface in an orgy of violent power.

The lingering effects of the Varlian Device saturated the ground. Most Daemons would have found such psychic fallout intolerable, but these lords of ruin were mighty indeed. Worshipped as fell deities by some, they had enslaved empires and corrupted entire sub-sectors. As Waersk regrouped his shattered court, the Daemons pounced on his Knight Despoiler, Khorifex. They sank into its chassis, welding every vent and hatch shut with

infernal fire. Waersk screamed in horror as the essences possessed the Throne Mechanicum he was linked to, tearing out the imprinted spirits and casting them into the warp. Khorifex's structure mutated, piercing its master with iron shards. Waersk desperately pleaded with the Daemons, offering them the service of his court. Cackling peals of laughter poured into his skull in response, as a blemish in the air between Khorifex and the Chaos Knights of his court swelled into a bottomless vortex. One by one, the traitor war engines were dragged into it, taking their Fallen Nobles with them.

The four daemonic essences were not yet done with this world. They beheld the rising flares of mass conveyors returning to high orbit, and tracked the trail of null-energy back to the Adeptus Mechanicus ships. The most far-sighted of the essences told its brothers that more of the fearsome devices would appear if they ignored these mortals, and with a thought the creatures sped towards the Martian vessels, a call of summons rippling through the warp as they went.

The remaining Adeptus Mechanicus ships of Kroll's Reclamation Fleet were in uproar. The Magos had dumped an emergency data-packet into their data-core containing his observations of the device's effects, but it came with the revelation of his abduction by Baroness Sordhen. When warp breaches appeared on the decks of each ship, therefore, the remaining Skitarii clades were already on a war footing.

The vast hangar bay of Kroll's flagship, the *Regulus Prime*, stretched for a mile along its spine. There Vanguard and Ranger squads waited in rigidly delineated areas as hundreds of servitors made ready assault craft to reclaim their Magos from the Knights. But without warning, eight spatial anomalies burst into being within the hangar, and from their eternal depths crawled gangling creatures of changing hues, their skin alight with unnatural fire.

Searing bolts of flame lashed out at witless servitors as canisters of promethium exploded in pink-tinged fireballs. The Skitarii Alphas requested doctrines from the

```
<<Vox echo 77.rt9, est. origin
Soelich Sub-sector. Meta: Voltoris'
Spear+
/--Addendum: Further clarity on
signal location cannot be provided.
Monitoring of warp anomaly expansion
[cf. file 21Σ, 'Siren's Storm']
reveals emergence of Thark waveforms.
Consequently, Your Majesty, no
timestamp exists for this fragment.
```

bridge as Daemons flooded the enormous hangar and fires raged uncontrollably. In the cavernous ceiling space, soaring razor-edged Daemons and squads of Pteraxii hunted each other amongst the forest of gantries and macro-cranes.

In the bowels of the *Regulus Prime*, the bloated Magos Jabek fiercely organised the defence of the enginarium. Permanently sealed into a gargantuan suspended platform from which he controlled everything in his domain, the Magos sent gangs of indentured labourers to shield his precious generatoria, Geller field housings and power couplings from the filth-encrusted creatures spewing from the warp breaches.

To Magos Jabek's horror and disgust, several of the work gangs defending the Geller field had sprouted biomechanical appendages seeping with brackish filth, and now tore at the machinery's housing with rasping claws. Smoking brass blades effortlessly severed Jabek's Kataphron retinue into pieces before a bestial winged shadow dropped down with a roar upon the Magos' exposed platform.

The desperate Magi on the bridge futilely attempted to collate similar reports from each of their ships. Hundreds of localised warp breaches had materialised throughout the fleet, and creatures defying categorisation were emerging in droves to revel in blood-fuelled slaughter. The bridge's arched gateway was sealed, but a purple-hued breach manifested in

the centre of the control dais. From it leapt blurred shapes, pale and barbed, which eviscerated the hard-wired command crew in a matter of moments. Binharic blurts for aid squalled in unison, then expired. The master of this daemonic host languidly approached the shipmaster and drove its long talons through his body, feeding its

essence into the ship's navigational controls. Couched in the *Regulus Prime*'s command protocols, an order bled outwards to the other ships. As one, the Adeptus Mechanicus fleet turned and powered towards the fiery heart of the system's star.

'[signal distortion] —n't blame her, not for leading us out of that hell of traps and deceit. Terra, you should have seen her fight! It was like on the tapestries in His Majesty's weapons chamber. When the Baroness tore the Throne from one and then hurled it at the next, the setting sun clipped the cowling on Bright Destroyer's carapace. The Emperor himself was there that day, g— [mask 4.0 degradation] her arm, guiding us all. I felt him when that damnable… chill took us.

You know I was with her when she took Kroll? "Lady Mairi," she asked me, as calm as a glacier, even as his guard were peppering us with irradiated shot and he squirmed like a broken toy in her grasp. "Explain to them that they can return to their ships, or they can die. The choice is binary." I couldn't have kept that calm, I couldn't have kept from crushing him after what he'd done. There are some left, but so many voices in the Thrones are gone, I'll never hear them again.'

Echoes of Awakening

The Great Rift blights the skies of every world in the galaxy, imprinting a ragged blemish onto the eyes and minds of any who dare look upon it. Fears, omens and rabid hysteria clog vox-nets and shattered astropathic ducts as terror grips Humanity. To those who listen, their individual significance melds into a greater whole and a terrible new age begins to crystallise.

+++

I swear by the Chain-psalm of Holy Fusion, this is accurate! The Lodge of Truspark has been approached by fellow seekers. Yes! No, I have no idea which forge they hail from, but monitor my words, they have found a holy STC! One that can help. We have been selected from amongst the entire priesthood to test it. The Magos is proposing a Reclamation Fleet to the Fabricator Locum as cover. This is Metalica's chance to shine brighter than Mars. It is a unique device, the only one in existence.

+++

Interview 1d with Astropath Dhe Vhoolian Ri, Ty Precinct House, pending arrest and interr. on advice of [REDACTED], of Fort [Auth .1k]

What business is it of the Sector Arbitrators anyway? It was just a ghost tale. They were the first ship we'd come across in three months. Sol Tegrel isn't a Trader who cares for busy… that is, he's just a careful man. The other Trader had invited Sol to a glass of something. He took a few of us and, well, they're a bunch of foul-mouths, so I sought out their Astropath. No, constable, we just speak, it's easier. Well, he told me of a roaring he'd heard under almost every sending towards Morsh. Voices, beast noises, he said, like a thousand mating theyghorles – no, I don't either – but it had frightened him, because a month earlier he'd heard echoes of roaring and chanting through the Burgu Strait. Of course, I just had to tell him about the terrible roars I'd endured only a day before. Oh, I can't rememb— well, yes, but how did you know?

+++

Cry your red tears and scar yourself if it helps. When the pale-kin come to play there will be time for nothing as boring as tears!

+++

[Intercepted transmission — astr. duct Regia Kappa 7c.88]
Security Protocol H.3.91uu

'It is too late for us now, I feel sure. Some threshold has been reached. In the past, the glow of Panna Magna that my mind perceived would wax and wane as the Sensitive multiplied in hidden lairs and the Governor purged them. Now, their shining witchlight is almost all I can see. In the Emperor's name, I beg you, warn anyone you can. Tell them not to come near this system! We have fallen.'

Recommend immediate sector quarantine. Redirect inbound assets 2c - V33.

+++

Passive monitoring notification Beta 3Ω, Vulgis Barracks, Jaker V

Guardsmen, this is for Humanity. I know none of you take up arms lightly. But remember, we are not against Jaker. The colonists have promised this will remain our world. Let us end the meeting in prayer.

For the benefit of all.

For the benefit of all. [vox relay suggests repetition by 63 identified enlisted voices]

+ + //Jaker Commissariat advised. Penal indenture recommended following prejudicial termination.

+++

Waheka Garrison, timestamp 3r.22.1-a, reg. chapel vox-lift

We've been buried in this nightmare for three weeks. The platoon's lho stick ration lasted just one. Saint's bones, the stuff we've seen; mates ripped inside out, faces in the sky and… the thing that crawled out of the Wyrd. I don't care what we have to do, or who we execute. I just want this stuff to stop!

He never went far enough, your corpse-god. There were secrets to master, but he was too afraid. You can help me reach far further.

Final transmission received by Rejuvenat sanatoria barque *Zygocyte Imperator*, found wrecked.

+++

```
[vox-thief μV-4.{p}9, deck 376h,
holding cell 55.1, Voltoris' Spear]
```

'Do you realise what you've done? Most of those suits were of my Household, their Nobles my kin! They had more honour in an actuator pin than in your entire foul carcass— [repeated strikes of solid object into assumed fracturing mechanism]. Mechanicus, repair thyself, I dare you!'

```
++[broken vox] -ess, Baroness, you
are not in possession of the relevant
data.++
```

'Nothing you cant will save your hide. Do your own vows mean nothing, traitor? Holy Throne, Kroll, you will burn for this. I imagine Mars will petition the High King for your full sensory inload too, so they can take their pound of flesh from you themselves! Bondsman, administer the coil again, and increase the setting.'

```
++Attend, Baroness, I- [multi-layered
binharic broadcast, no correlation to
known Mars info-crypt] Sor- [broken
vox] honoured Lady Terryn, it worked! I
can block the warp!++
```

'Do not manipulate me, Tech-Priest. Even your own kind left you behind, they were so ashamed of your deeds. Your falsehoods have damned you…'

```
++It is the truth! Pure empirical
truth, I can prove it! The device
severed the citadel's connection with
the warp. It was only temporary, there
is calibr-++
```

'That is impossible. Do not take me for a fool. Witchcraft is severed through steel and fire. It must be rooted out. Bondsman, adminis-'

```
++Attend! It is the truth, by the
Omnissiah! It can be fabricated
to greater tolerances. It… it
will be shared with House Terryn.
The means to kill every psy-
every witch will be yours.++

++Baroness, I th-++
```

'Show me.'

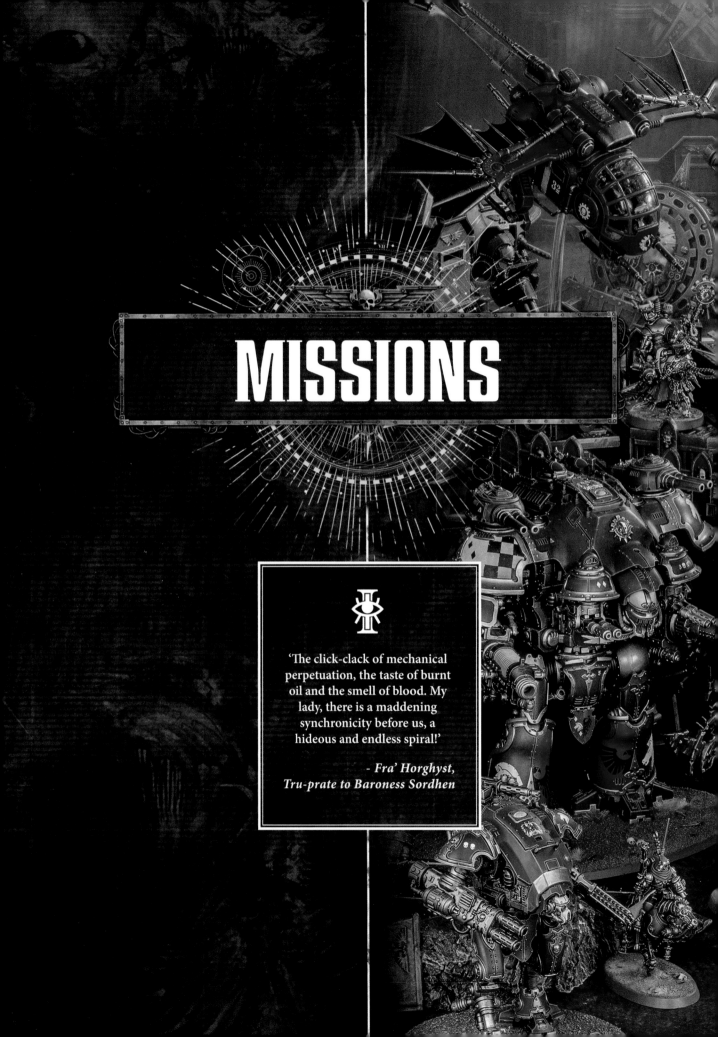

MISSIONS

'The click-clack of mechanical perpetuation, the taste of burnt oil and the smell of blood. My lady, there is a maddening synchronicity before us, a hideous and endless spiral!'

- *Fra' Horghyst,*
Tru-prate to Baroness Sordhen

DIABOLICAL FIEFS

The rules presented on the following pages allow you to play games set in locations inspired by those found in the narrative of this book, as well as play through one of the most daring moments from the Siege of the Qysberg, where the Imperial Knights breached the citadel's walls and faced its monstrous Chaos Knight lords and a series of hellish traps. Will you fight alongside the noble warriors of the Padah March to cleanse Ordex-Thaag, or will you cruelly crush the interlopers to protect the grand scheme to widen the Siren's Storm?

INTRODUCTION

This section starts by providing a new Theatre of War, shown opposite, that is designed to represent any one of the numerous battlefields across Ordex-Thaag. Whilst the nefarious entities that reside beneath the surface might not march to war themselves, their presence can still be felt in the dangerous and unpredictable fumaroles across the planet.

These rules can, however, be used and modified to represent any location where activity beneath a planet's surface has an impact on the battlefields above. This could be the machinations of an awakening tomb world mobilising for war, or the effects of Tyranids burrowing through a volcanic death world.

On pages 24-25, a new historical battle is presented for use in narrative play. Breaching the Qysberg lets players fight through the heroic assault of the Imperial Knights on the Chaos Knights fortress. The mission describes how to lay out the battlefield in order to best reflect this specific battlefront, and provides new rules and Stratagems for use in this scenario. It is particularly suited to battles involving Chaos Knights and/or Imperial Knights, providing new cover rules to represent the titanic duels between these mighty war engines.

THEATRES OF WAR

Deep within the core of Ordex-Thaag, the Daemon-splicers of the Dark Mechanicum have bound tortured warp essences in their schemes to tear a new Great Rift into being. Their loathsome machineries have spread poisonous and fracturing energies out to the surface and none now can escape their touch.

These rules are designed to reflect the impact of the Dark Mechanicum's presence in the core of Ordex-Thaag as their Daemon forges function and their despicable designs come to fruition. They can, however, be used to represent any circumstance in which nefarious forces operate beneath the battlefield. They are entirely optional and, so long as you and your opponent agree, can be used in any Warhammer 40,000 game, set anywhere.

THEATRE OF WAR: HAZARDOUS FUMAROLES

The planet harbours an evil in its depths, its presence working to produce vile energy and twisted abominations. Across the surface, evidence of their potency can be found in hazardous fumaroles and tectonic rumblings, as well as wellsprings of poisonous and savage emanations.

Fumaroles

After setting up terrain, but before determining deployment zones and/or setting up armies, the players roll off. Starting with the winner, the players take it in turns to set up one fumarole marker until six have been set up. Each marker can be placed anywhere on the battlefield more than 12" from the edge of the battlefield and any other fumarole marker.

At the start of the first battle round but before the first turn begins, the player taking the first turn rolls one D6 for each fumarole marker and consults the following table to establish the effects of that fumarole marker. Place a dice on that fumarole marker that corresponds to the result to remind you of its effects.

D6	RESULT
1	**Escaped Predatory Sentience:** At the end of their turn, each player rolls one D6 for each unit from their army within 3" of the centre of this marker. On a 3+, that unit suffers D3 mortal wounds.
2	**Smog:** When resolving an attack made with a ranged weapon against a unit wholly within 6" of the centre of this marker, subtract 1 from the hit roll. When resolving an attack made with a ranged weapon by a model within 6" of the centre of this marker, subtract 1 from the hit roll.
3	**Toxic Waste:** Whilst a unit is within 3" of the centre of this marker, subtract 1 from the Toughness characteristic of all models in that unit.
4	**Steam:** Whilst a unit is within 3" of the centre of this marker, subtract 1 from the Strength characteristic of all models in that unit. Whilst a unit is within 3" of the centre of this marker, when resolving an attack made with a melee weapon by a model in that unit, subtract 1 from the hit roll.
5	**Sinkhole:** Unless it is TITANIC or can FLY, a model gains the benefit of cover to its saving throw whilst its unit is wholly within 6" of the centre of this marker. Unless the unit can FLY, if a unit makes a charge move and any of its models wish to move within 6" of the centre of this marker, subtract 2 from the charge roll (to a minimum of 0).
6	**Psychic Run-off:** When a Psychic test or Deny the Witch test is taken for a unit within 3" of the centre of this marker, you can re-roll one of the dice. If a unit suffers Perils of the Warp whilst within 3" of the centre of this marker, when inflicting mortal wounds on that unit, roll one additional dice and discard the lowest result.

Dark Presence

At the start of each battle round, roll one D3 on the following table:

D3	RESULT
1	**Brief Respite:** No additional effect until the end of the battle round.
2	**Accelerated Production:** Randomly select one fumarole marker. Until the end of the battle round, add 3" to the range of that marker's effects.
3	**Rumble in the Deep:** Until the end of the battle round, subtract 1 from the Move characteristic of all models unless they can FLY. Subtract 1 from Advance and charge rolls made for all units unless they can FLY.

ECHOES OF WAR
BREACHING THE QYSBERG

Having broken through the fortified gatehouse of the vast Qysberg citadel, Imperial Knights rush across the breach to engage their traitor counterparts. The battle quickly descends into a ruthless melee where titanic murder is all either side cares for. But the Qysberg itself remains a treacherous foe.

THE ARMIES

Each player must first muster an army from their collection. The Attacker commands the Imperial Knights that have breached the Qysberg. The Defender commands the Chaos Knights defending it. A player can include any models in their army, but this mission is most suited to armies that only contain **Imperial Knights** and **Chaos Knights**. If a player's army is Battle-forged, they will also be able to use the appropriate Stratagems included with this mission (see opposite).

THE BATTLEFIELD

Create the battlefield using the deployment map below and set up terrain. There should be ruins, buildings and larger terrain features (each of which is ideally at least 4" tall at its highest point) scattered across the battlefield, ensuring the distance between each terrain feature is enough so that each model in the players' armies can move between the terrain features. In addition, there should be no terrain features within the Attacker's deployment zone.

DEPLOYMENT

The Attacker deploys their army wholly within their deployment zone. Any models that cannot be deployed are placed in reserve. They cannot make use of any rules that allow them to set up in any other location. The Defender then deploys their army wholly within their deployment zone.

FIRST TURN

The Attacker has the first turn.

THROUGH THE BREACH

At the end of the Attacker's Movement phase, they can set up any models from their army that are in reserve wholly within their deployment zone. Any models that cannot be set up this way remain in reserve. Models from the Defender's army cannot be set up or finish any kind of move within the Attacker's deployment zone.

TITANIC DUELS

When resolving an attack made with a ranged weapon against an **Imperial Knights** or **Chaos Knights** unit, the target receives the benefit of cover to its saving throw if a straight line 1mm in width cannot be drawn from the centre of the attacking model's base to the centre of the target's base without crossing over or through a terrain feature. In addition, when resolving an attack made with a ranged weapon against an **Imperial Knights** or **Chaos Knights** unit, subtract 1 from the hit roll if a straight line 1mm in width cannot be drawn from the centre of the attacking model's base to any part of the target's base without crossing over or through a terrain feature.

BATTLE LENGTH

At the end of battle round 5, the Attacker rolls one D6. On a 3+, the game continues, otherwise the game is over. At the end of battle round 6, the Defender rolls one D6. On a 4+, the game continues, otherwise the game is over. The battle automatically ends at the end of battle round 7.

VICTORY CONDITIONS

At the end of the battle, each player adds up the Power Ratings or points values of units from their opponent's army that have been destroyed. If a unit has not been destroyed at the end of the battle but has lost more than half of its models, or a single-model unit has lost more than half its wounds, add half the Power Rating or points value of that unit (rounding up) to the opponent's total. The player with the highest total wins. If the totals are the same, the battle is a draw.

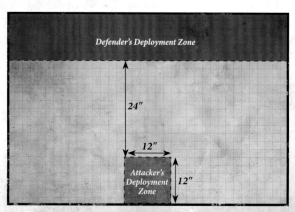

STRATAGEMS

In this mission, the players can use Command Points (CPs) to use the following bonus Stratagems:

STORM THE CITADEL!

1CP

Attacker Stratagem

Filled with the religious zeal of Baroness Sordhen, the Imperial Knights would allow nothing to stay their fury.

Use this Stratagem in your Movement phase, when you declare an **IMPERIAL KNIGHTS** model from your army will Advance. Until the end of the turn, when making an Advance roll for that model, roll two additional D6 and discard two of the dice. Until the end of the turn, that model can shoot with ranged weapons as if it had not Advanced.

OVERLAPPING ION DEFENCE

2CP

Attacker Stratagem

To weather the concentrated defensive fire, the Imperial Knights of the Padah March overlapped their ion shields.

Use this Stratagem when an **IMPERIAL KNIGHTS** unit from your army is chosen as the target of an attack made with a ranged weapon whilst within 2" of another friendly **IMPERIAL KNIGHTS** unit. Until the start of your next turn, when resolving an attack made with a ranged weapon against that targeted unit or any friendly **IMPERIAL KNIGHTS** units within 2" of that unit, add 1 to the saving throw. You can only use this Stratagem once per battle.

UNSHEATHING THE LANCE

1CP

Attacker Stratagem

Moving in fluid coordination, Imperial Knights lanced forward from the lee of their oath-sworn fellows.

Use this Stratagem in your Charge phase, when you choose an **IMPERIAL KNIGHTS** model from your army to charge with whilst within 2" of another friendly **IMPERIAL KNIGHTS** model. Until the end of the turn, you can re-roll charge rolls made for that model and when resolving an attack made with a melee weapon by that model, you can re-roll the wound roll.

KILLZONE CRUELTY

1CP

Defender Stratagem

Catching their foes in perfect killzones, the Chaos Knights employed potent enfilading fire from titanic embrasures.

Use this Stratagem in your Shooting phase, when a **CHAOS KNIGHTS** model from your army is chosen to shoot with. Until the end of the phase, when resolving an attack made by that model against a unit wholly within the Attacker's deployment zone, re-roll a wound roll of 1.

PREDATORY TECHNOVIRUS

1CP

Defender Stratagem

Within the Qysberg's seemingly archaic foundations were enervating technoviruses preying on specific systems.

Use this Stratagem at the end of your opponent's Movement phase. Select one weapon equipped by a model from your opponent's army that is within 3" of a terrain feature. Until the end of the turn, when resolving an attack made with that weapon by that model, half the Strength characteristic of that attack.

ENGINE KILL-SNARE

2CP

Defender Stratagem

The Chaos Knights had rigged their domain with deadly and esoteric traps primed to maim invading engines.

Use this Stratagem at the start of your opponent's Movement phase. Select one terrain feature, then select one point on the battlefield within 6" of that terrain feature and more than 1" away from any enemy models. Draw an imaginary line, 1mm wide, between that point on the battlefield and the closest part of that terrain feature. Until the end of the turn, each time a **VEHICLE** unit moves onto or through that line, it suffers D6 mortal wounds.

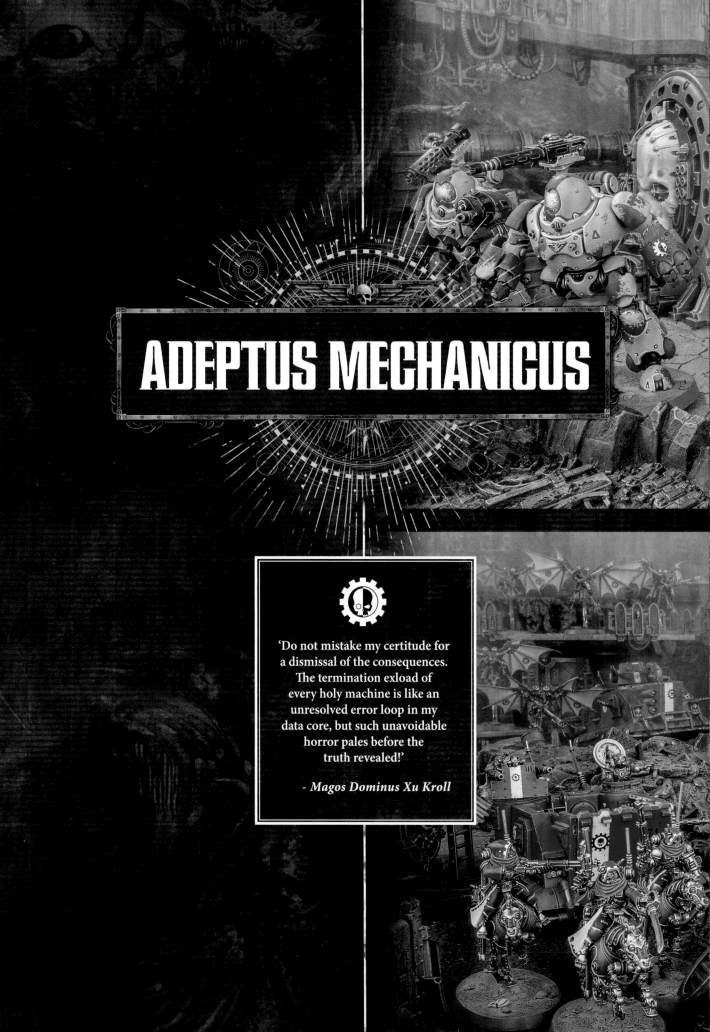

ADEPTUS MECHANICUS

'Do not mistake my certitude for a dismissal of the consequences. The termination exload of every holy machine is like an unresolved error loop in my data core, but such unavoidable horror pales before the truth revealed!'

- *Magos Dominus Xu Kroll*

KEEPERS OF DIVINE LORE

The rules in this section supplement those found in *Codex: Adeptus Mechanicus* and can be used in any open play, narrative play or matched play game. They include new units, Warlord Traits, Stratagems, Canticles and rules for creating your own forge world dogmas.

New Units

Pages 31-43 present new units for the forces of the Adeptus Mechanicus. You will find a detailed account of their background and fighting style, followed by datasheets to use these new units in your games of Warhammer 40,000.

Holy Order Warlord Traits

Pages 46-47 feature new Warlord Traits representing the capabilities of the devotees of each of four Holy Orders of the Omnissiah.

Stratagems

If your army is Battle-forged and includes any **Adeptus Mechanicus** Detachments, the Stratagems on pages 48-49 can be used in addition to those presented in *Codex: Adeptus Mechanicus*.

Forge World Dogmas

Most of the forces of the Adeptus Mechanicus belong to a forge world. This is represented by the <**Forge World**> keyword. Pages 50-51 present a selection of abilities that can be combined to create a forge world of your own devising, or to represent one from the Warhammer 40,000 background that is not represented by a forge world dogma in *Codex: Adeptus Mechanicus*.

Forge World Canticles

Page 52 contains a number of Canticles of the Omnissiah that are specific to each of the named forge worlds found within *Codex: Adeptus Mechanicus*. These can be used to better represent the forces of those forge worlds on the tabletop.

Name Generator

Page 53 provides a useful tool to help you name your Adeptus Mechanicus warriors, further building the background and personality of your army.

Arc Weapons: An arc weapon is any weapon whose profile includes the word 'arc' (arc rifle, heavy arc rifle, arc maul, etc.), and any Relic that replaces such a weapon.

Radium Weapons: A radium weapon is any weapon whose profile includes the word 'radium' (radium carbine, radium pistol, etc.), and any Relic that replaces such a weapon.

Cognis Weapons: A cognis weapon is any weapon whose profile includes the word 'cognis' (cognis flamer, twin cognis lascannon, etc.), and any Relic that replaces such a weapon.

SERVANTS OF THE MACHINE GOD

The dogmatic, techno-religious orders of the Adeptus Mechanicus are geared towards the veneration of knowledge embodied by the Machine God. Overseen by cloistered cabals of Tech-Priests, the armies of their sovereign forge worlds maintain macroclades of cyborg warriors and arcane engines of war.

TECH-PRIESTS MANIPULUS

The ruling castes of the Adeptus Mechanicus are the Tech-Priests, robed zealots whose flesh is replaced over time with bionic enhancements. These techno-savants carry a bewildering array of titles, and each one specialises in arcane knowledge and esoteric lore, perpetuated with religious fervour.

Within the bulbous augmentation of a Tech-Priest Manipulus is a galvanic cell, from which they can channel a powerful charge of divine Motive Force – the underlying current of all life. Tech-Priests Manipulus eagerly seek out new sources of power, draining them dry with their mechadendrites. Filled with thrumming potential, they empower the servants of the Machine God and the holy creations of war they bear. The Tech-Priest Manipulus' electropositors overcharge servos, energise weapon cells and invigorate cerebral cores. Saturated with the pure power of the Machine God, the mortal warriors and sacred engines carry his praise forward as they cast the heretics down.

SERBERYS CAVALRY

To be promoted from the Skitarii maniples to the Serberys corps is a great honour. They ride swift quadrupedal constructs whose razor-clawed limbs allow them to manoeuvre easily over the most shattered terrain, while their riders are mag-locked in gyro-stabilised positions.

Serberys Raiders are long-range scouts and outriders. They excel at outflanking enemy forces and picking off unprotected assets. Advanced ocular arrays implanted into the riders' skulls are noospherically linked with their mounts, ensuring maximum accuracy, while finely calibrated olfactory sensors and a suite of sensitive augury equipment make them dogged and feared trackers.

The incandescent flash of phosphor and the stench of charred flesh surround Serberys Sulphurhounds. Appointed from some of the most aggressive Skitarii clades, within their forge world's temples they patrol lumen-lit enclosures as fell guardians, while on the battlefield, they are shock line breakers. Once released by their Tech-Priest masters they smash into, then through, defensive positions before circling back for any survivors.

SKORPIUS ARMOURED VEHICLES

The bone-jarring din of thrumming engines and the billowing wake of fluorescent smog heralds the deployment of a forge world's hover tanks and transports. A cushion of hyper-reactive gas impels these angular war engines over hazardous terrain, while the pressure wave beneath them hammers the land flat.

The majority of forge worlds exist as toxic wastelands – the result of millennia of industrial overproduction – and the Skorpius-pattern chassis was developed to traverse these planets' acidic bogs. Beneath a pressurised skirt of toughened nanofibre, alchemical gas is atomised by half-forgotten processes, creating forward impulse and belching a backwash of fumes.

SKORPIUS DISINTEGRATORS

Bristling with heavy weapons, Skorpius Disintegrators are fast-moving battle tanks. Whether individually supporting advances or thrusting forward in dozens-strong tides, Skorpius Disintegrators keep up a blistering rate of fire and deadly payloads. Salvoes of missiles are launched in pre-programmed waves, and the heavy clunk of reloading is heard even before the first detonations. The tank's primary armament varies. Some carry a belleros energy cannon, its arcing projectiles using the same hyper-reactive gas as the hover drives, but super-heated and reinjected; the projectile explodes on impact in a seething, spectroscopic energy blast. Others bear a ferrumite cannon, whose thudding, solid-core shells become molten spears upon contact, flash-heating whatever they impale.

SKORPIUS DUNERIDERS

More radical Tech-Priests risk the wrath of the Skorpius Dunerider's machine spirit by using the rugged vehicle for long-range transport. More often, lines of Skorpius Duneriders travel behind marching cohorts of Skitarii, the warriors' optics eerily glowing through the vehicles' fumes as they advance in lockstep.

Skorpius Duneriders are calibrated for the swift delivery of front-line assets into the heart of battle. In clouds of dust and tendrils of chemical smoke, they sweep upon enemy defences or into designated fire points. Their armoured ramp slams down and from within stride the cybernetic and heavily augmented warriors of the Machine God, while the Skorpius Dunerider pours heavy calibre shot into the foe from its cognis heavy stubbers.

AIRBORNE ASSETS

There is no sphere of knowledge or theatre of war that can escape the reach of the Omnissiah and his devotees. Above a forge world's ground forces, preternatural amalgams of biomass and bionics hunt their prey and raptorial aircraft glide and manoeuvre over the twisting thermals of war and ruin.

PTERAXII

One of many specialised castes of cyborg warriors available to the Adeptus Mechanicus, the Pteraxii are optimised for instinctive reaction and agility. Pteraxii's reflexes are accentuated by paring back elements of cogitation that impede their primary function. Implanted with additional limb-stumps – scapuli superior – on their back, a flight pack of thrusters and reactive life surfaces is connected to them. The flight packs become part of the Pteraxii, who serve in several roles.

Sterylizors, for example, are honed for aggression, and their legs end in vicious, spur-like talons. They scour cavernous forge temples free of technosites and cyblight infestations and Tech-Priests do not hesitate to turn the Sterylizors' phosphor torches on intelligent adversaries. Skystalkers, meanwhile, find optimal vantage points from which to pick off their targets – whether isolated battlefield marks or feral psyber familiars and servo-cherubim – with flurries of razor-sharp flechettes.

ARCHAEOPTERS

A workhorse not only of the toxic Martian skies, but of distant worlds at the forefront of the Tech-Priests' expansion for millennia, the Archaeopter is an agile, fixed-wing aircraft. Piloted by a member of the Pteraxii caste whose legs and scapuli superior are hardwired into its controls, the nano-carbon fibre-weave of the Archaeopter's wings is capable of morphing – a property it shares with Pteraxii flight packs. This affords great manoeuvrability and enables it to operate within changing pressures.

The Archaeopter's ancient design was eventually deemed holy enough to accommodate sub-roles. Archaeopter Transvectors undertake explorator duties, as well as delivering teams of lethal operatives behind enemy lines or into the heart of battle. From an ordnance selector, Archaeopter Fusilaves drop payloads of ground-penetrating, tectomagnic bombs that cause seismic shock waves, while Archaeopter Stratoraptors saturate the foe with fire from their fearsome array of armaments.

TECH-PRIEST MANIPULUS

NAME	M	WS	BS	S	T	W	A	Ld	Sv
Tech-Priest Manipulus	6"	3+	3+	4	4	4	3	8	2+

A Tech-Priest Manipulus is a single model equipped with: magnarail lance; mechadendrites; Omnissian staff.

WEAPON	RANGE	TYPE	S	AP	D	ABILITIES
Magnarail lance	18"	Heavy 1	7	-3	D3	When resolving an attack made with this weapon, if the bearer remained stationary in its previous Movement phase, this weapon has a Damage characteristic of 3 for that attack.
Transonic cannon	8"	Assault D6	4	-1	2	When resolving an attack made with this weapon, do not make a hit roll: it automatically scores a hit.
Mechadendrites	Melee	Melee	User	0	1	When the bearer fights, it makes D6 additional attacks with this weapon.
Omnissian staff	Melee	Melee	+2	-1	2	-

WARGEAR OPTIONS	• This model can be equipped with 1 transonic cannon instead of 1 magnarail lance.

ABILITIES

Canticles of the Omnissiah (see *Codex: Adeptus Mechanicus*)

Blessed Bionics: This model has a 5+ invulnerable save. At the start of your Movement phase, this model regains up to D3 lost wounds.

Master of Machines: At the end of your Movement phase, this model can repair one other friendly <**Forge World**> or **Questor Mechanicus** model within 3" of it. If the model being repaired is a <**Forge World**> model, it regains up to D3 lost wounds; if it is a **Questor Mechanicus** model, it regains up to 1 lost wound. Each model can only be repaired by the Master of Machines ability once per turn.

Galvanic Field: At the start of your Movement phase, select one of the abilities below. This model gains that ability until the start of your next Movement phase:

• **Bolster Warriors:** Add 1" to the Move characteristic of <**Forge World**> units whilst they are within 6" of any friendly models with this ability. Add 1 to Advance rolls and charge rolls made for <**Forge World**> units whilst they are within 6" of any friendly models with this ability.

• **Bolster Weapons:** This model cannot move for any reason. Add 6" to the maximum Range characteristic of ranged weapons with an unmodified Range characteristic of 24" or more that are equipped by models in <**Forge World**> units whilst they are within 6" of any friendly models with this ability. Add 2" to the maximum Range characteristic of all other ranged weapons models in <**Forge World**> units are equipped with whilst they are within 6" of any friendly models with this ability.

FACTION KEYWORDS	IMPERIUM, ADEPTUS MECHANICUS, CULT MECHANICUS, <FORGE WORLD>
KEYWORDS	CHARACTER, INFANTRY, TECH-PRIEST, MANIPULUS

'Terra's mutants – her Astropaths, her Navigators, her "investigators" – like to proselytise their nonsense about the power of psychic potential. They prattle that its strength runs through all life, that yoked to the Imperium's will it will deliver our enemies.

Mars has always known of the true strength in the universe. The Machine God's manifestation as the Motive Force, the vitality of its servants – both mechanical and biological – is self evident. What power lies in the minds of psykers is fuelled ultimately, fundamentally, by the Motive Force. Ave Mechanicus!'

- Tech-Priest Manipulus Rhovanordie 31.7/c G'ant, Nunc Mechanicus to the Adeptus Astra Telepathica

SERBERYS SULPHURHOUNDS

NAME	M	WS	BS	S	T	W	A	Ld	Sv
Serberys Sulphurhound	12"	4+	3+	3	3	3	1	6	4+
Serberys Sulphurhound Alpha	12"	4+	3+	3	3	3	2	7	4+

This unit contains 1 Serberys Sulphurhound Alpha and 2 Serberys Sulphurhounds. It can additionally contain up to 3 Serberys Sulphurhounds (**Power Rating +3**) or up to 6 Serberys Sulphurhounds (**Power Rating +6**). The Serberys Sulphurhound Alpha is equipped with: phosphor blast pistol; sulphur breath; clawed limbs; power maul. Every Serberys Sulphurhound is equipped with: 2 phosphor pistols; sulphur breath; clawed limbs.

WEAPON	RANGE	TYPE	S	AP	D	ABILITIES
Phosphor blast carbine	24"	Assault 4	5	-1	1	When resolving an attack made with this weapon, the target does not receive the benefit of cover.
Phosphor blast pistol	12"	Pistol 1	5	-1	1	When resolving an attack made with this weapon, the target does not receive the benefit of cover.
Phosphor pistol	12"	Pistol 1	4	-1	1	When resolving an attack made with this weapon, the target does not receive the benefit of cover.
Sulphur breath	8"	Pistol D6	4	-1	1	When resolving an attack made with this weapon, do not make a hit roll: it automatically scores a hit. In addition, the target does not receive the benefit of cover.
Clawed limbs	Melee	Melee	+1	0	1	When the bearer fights, it makes 2 additional attacks with this weapon.
Power maul	Melee	Melee	+2	-1	1	-

WARGEAR OPTIONS	• For every 3 models this unit contains, one Serberys Sulphurhound can be equipped with 1 phosphor blast carbine instead of 1 phosphor pistol.

ABILITIES	**Canticles of the Omnissiah** (see *Codex: Adeptus Mechanicus*) **Pistoleers:** You can choose to fire Pistol weapons models in this unit are equipped with, even if this unit Advanced this turn.	**Rad-saturation:** Subtract 1 from the Toughness characteristic of enemy units without the **VEHICLE** keyword whilst they are within 1" of any units from your army with this ability. **Bionics:** Models in this unit have a 6+ invulnerable save.

FACTION KEYWORDS	**IMPERIUM, ADEPTUS MECHANICUS, SKITARII, <FORGE WORLD>**
KEYWORDS	**CAVALRY, SERBERYS SULPHURHOUNDS**

The muzzles of Sulphurhounds' mounts have been adapted to release a sulphur breath.

Serberys Sulphurhound with two phosphor pistols

Serberys Sulphurhound Alpha with phosphor blast pistol and power maul

SERBERYS RAIDERS

NAME	M	WS	BS	S	T	W	A	Ld	Sv
Serberys Raider	12"	4+	3+	3	3	3	1	6	4+
Serberys Raider Alpha	12"	4+	3+	3	3	3	2	7	4+

This unit contains 1 Serberys Raider Alpha and 2 Serberys Raiders. It can additionally contain up to 3 Serberys Raiders (**Power Rating +2**) or up to 6 Serberys Raiders (**Power Rating +4**). The Serberys Raider Alpha is equipped with: archeo-revolver; galvanic carbine; cavalry sabre; clawed limbs. Every Serberys Raider is equipped with: galvanic carbine; cavalry sabre; clawed limbs.

WEAPON	RANGE	TYPE	S	AP	D	ABILITIES
Archeo-revolver	12"	Pistol 1	5	-2	2	-
Galvanic carbine	18"	Assault 2	4	0	1	When resolving an attack made with this weapon, on an unmodified wound roll of 6 this weapon has an Armour Penetration characteristic of -1 for that attack.
Cavalry sabre	Melee	Melee	+1	-1	1	-
Clawed limbs	Melee	Melee	+1	0	1	When the bearer fights, it makes 2 additional attacks with this weapon.

WARGEAR OPTIONS	• One Serberys Raider can have an enhanced data-tether.

ABILITIES	**Canticles of the Omnissiah** (see *Codex: Adeptus Mechanicus*) **Bionics:** Models in this unit have a 6+ invulnerable save. **Skirmishing Line:** At the start of the first battle round, before the first turn begins, this unit can move as if it were your Movement phase. This unit must end that move more than 9" away from any enemy models. If both players have units that can do this, the player who is taking the first turn moves their units first.	**Eye of Serberys:** Ranged weapons models in this unit are equipped with can target a **Character** unit even if it is not the closest enemy unit. In addition, when resolving an attack made with a ranged weapon by a model in this unit, a wound roll of 6+ inflicts 1 mortal wound on the target in addition to any other damage. **Enhanced Data-tether:** If a model in this unit has an enhanced data-tether, you can re-roll Morale tests taken for this unit.

FACTION KEYWORDS	**IMPERIUM, ADEPTUS MECHANICUS, SKITARII, <FORGE WORLD>**
KEYWORDS	**CAVALRY, SERBERYS RAIDERS**

Serberys Raider with galvanic carbine and enhanced data-tether

Serberys Raider Alpha with archeo-revolver and cavalry sabre

PTERAXII STERYLIZORS

NAME	M	WS	BS	S	T	W	A	Ld	Sv
Pteraxii Sterylizor	12"	3+	3+	4	3	2	2	6	4+
Pteraxii Sterylizor Alpha	12"	3+	3+	4	3	2	3	7	4+

This unit contains 1 Pteraxii Sterylizor Alpha and 4 Pteraxii Sterylizors. It can additionally contain up to 5 Pteraxii Sterylizors (**Power Rating +4**). The Pteraxii Sterylizor Alpha is equipped with: flechette blaster; taser goad. Every Pteraxii Sterylizor is equipped with: phosphor torch; Pteraxii talons.

WEAPON	RANGE	TYPE	S	AP	D	ABILITIES
Flechette blaster	12"	Pistol 5	3	0	1	-
Phosphor torch	12"	Assault D6	4	-1	1	When resolving an attack made with this weapon, do not make a hit roll: it automatically scores a hit. In addition, the target does not receive the benefit of cover.
Pteraxii talons	Melee	Melee	User	-1	1	This weapon has a Strength characteristic of +1 if the bearer made a charge move or performed a Heroic Intervention this turn.
Taser goad	Melee	Melee	+2	0	1	When resolving an attack made with this weapon, an unmodified hit roll of 6 scores 2 additional hits.

ABILITIES	**Canticles of the Omnissiah** (see *Codex: Adeptus Mechanicus*) **Bionics:** Models in this unit have a 6+ invulnerable save. **Soar Away:** At the beginning of your Movement phase, this unit can boost into the skies. Remove this unit from the battlefield. It can return to the battlefield as described in the Thermal Riders ability. This unit cannot both soar away and descend in the same turn. If the battle ends while this unit is in the skies, this unit is considered to be destroyed.	**Thermal Riders:** During deployment, you can set up this unit in the skies instead of setting it up on the battlefield. If you do, or the unit has boosted into the skies using the Soar Away ability, at the end of one of your Movement phases you can set up this unit anywhere on the battlefield that is more than 9" away from any enemy models. **Swooping Strikes:** If this unit makes a charge move, add 1 to the Attacks characteristic of models in this unit until the end of the turn.
FACTION KEYWORDS	IMPERIUM, ADEPTUS MECHANICUS, SKITARII, <FORGE WORLD>	
KEYWORDS	INFANTRY, JUMP PACK, FLY, PTERAXII STERYLIZORS	

Pteraxii Sterylizor with phosphor torch

Pteraxii flight packs combine neuro-controlled wing surfaces and powerful propulsion

PTERAXII SKYSTALKERS

NAME	M	WS	BS	S	T	W	A	Ld	Sv
Pteraxii Skystalker	12"	3+	3+	4	3	2	2	6	4+
Pteraxii Skystalker Alpha	12"	3+	3+	4	3	2	3	7	4+

This unit contains 1 Pteraxii Skystalker Alpha and 4 Pteraxii Skystalkers. It can additionally contain up to 5 Pteraxii Skystalkers (**Power Rating +4**). The Pteraxii Skystalker Alpha is equipped with: flechette blaster; taser goad. Every Pteraxii Skystalker is equipped with: flechette carbine.

WEAPON	RANGE	TYPE		S	AP	D	ABILITIES
Flechette blaster	12"	Pistol 5		3	0	1	-
Flechette carbine	24"	Assault 5		3	0	1	-
Taser goad	Melee	Melee		+2	0	1	When resolving an attack made with this weapon, an unmodified hit roll of 6 scores 2 additional hits.

ABILITIES		
	Canticles of the Omnissiah (see *Codex: Adeptus Mechanicus*) **Bionics:** Models in this unit have a 6+ invulnerable save. **Soar Away:** At the beginning of your Movement phase, this unit can boost into the skies. Remove this unit from the battlefield. It can return to the battlefield as described in the Thermal Riders ability. This unit cannot both soar away and descend in the same turn. If the battle ends while this unit is in the skies, this unit is considered to be destroyed.	**Thermal Riders:** During deployment, you can set up this unit in the skies instead of setting it up on the battlefield. If you do, or the unit has boosted into the skies using the Soar Away ability, at the end of one of your Movement phases you can set up this unit anywhere on the battlefield that is more than 9" away from any enemy models. **Arc Grenade Cluster:** At the start of the Shooting phase you can select one enemy unit that this unit moved across this turn and roll one D6 for each model in this unit, adding 2 to each result if that unit is a **Vehicle**. For each 5+, that enemy unit suffers 1 mortal wound.

FACTION KEYWORDS	**IMPERIUM, ADEPTUS MECHANICUS, SKITARII, <FORGE WORLD>**
KEYWORDS	**INFANTRY, JUMP PACK, FLY, PTERAXII SKYSTALKERS**

Pteraxii Skystalker with flechette carbine

Claw-like appendages replace the Pteraxii's limbs .

Pteraxii Skystalker Alpha with flechette blaster and taser goad

SKORPIUS DUNERIDER

NAME	M	WS	BS	S	T	W	A	Ld	Sv
Skorpius Dunerider	*	6+	*	6	6	12	*	8	3+

DAMAGE

Some of this model's characteristics change as it suffers damage, as shown below:

REMAINING W	M	BS	A
7-12+	12"	3+	3
4-6	9"	4+	D3
1-3	6"	5+	1

A Skorpius Dunerider is a single model equipped with: 2 cognis heavy stubbers; twin cognis heavy stubber. It has a broad spectrum data-tether.

WEAPON	RANGE	TYPE	S	AP	D	ABILITIES
Cognis heavy stubber	36"	Heavy 3	4	0	1	You can choose this weapon to shoot with even if the bearer Advanced. When resolving an attack made with this weapon, if the bearer Advanced, subtract 2 from the hit roll.
Twin cognis heavy stubber	36"	Heavy 6	4	0	1	You can choose this weapon to shoot with even if the bearer Advanced. When resolving an attack made with this weapon, if the bearer Advanced, subtract 2 from the hit roll.

ABILITIES	**Canticles of the Omnissiah** (see *Codex: Adeptus Mechanicus*) **Broad Spectrum Data-tether:** At the start of the Morale phase, until the end of the phase, add 1 to the Leadership characteristic of **<Forge World>** models from your army if their unit is within 3" of any friendly models with a broad spectrum data-tether.	**Hover Platform:** This model does not suffer the penalty for moving and firing Heavy weapons. **Explodes:** When this model is destroyed, roll one D6 before any embarked models disembark, and before removing it from play. On a 6 it explodes, and each unit within 6" suffers D3 mortal wounds.
TRANSPORT	This model can transport 10 **Secutarii Infantry** or **<Forge World> Infantry** models. It cannot transport **Belisarius Cawl**, **Kataphron Breacher** or **Kataphron Destroyer** models.	
FACTION KEYWORDS	Imperium, Adeptus Mechanicus, Skitarii, <Forge World>	
KEYWORDS	Vehicle, Transport, Skorpius Dunerider	

SKORPIUS DISINTEGRATOR

NAME	M	WS	BS	S	T	W	A	Ld	Sv
Skorpius Disintegrator	*	6+	*	6	7	12	*	8	3+

DAMAGE

Some of this model's characteristics change as it suffers damage, as shown below:

REMAINING W	M	BS	A
7-12+	12"	3+	3
4-6	9"	4+	D3
1-3	6"	5+	1

A Skorpius Disintegrator is a single model equipped with: 3 cognis heavy stubbers; disruptor missile launcher; ferrumite cannon. It has a broad spectrum data-tether.

WEAPON	RANGE	TYPE	S	AP	D	ABILITIES
Belleros energy cannon	36"	Heavy 3D3	6	-1	2	This weapon can target units that are not visible to the bearer.
Cognis heavy stubber	36"	Heavy 3	4	0	1	You can choose this weapon to shoot with even if the bearer Advanced. When resolving an attack made with this weapon, if the bearer Advanced, subtract 2 from the hit roll.
Disruptor missile launcher	36"	Heavy D6	7	-2	D3	-
Ferrumite cannon	48"	Heavy 3	8	-3	3	-

WARGEAR OPTIONS	• This model can be equipped with 1 belleros energy cannon instead of 1 ferrumite cannon.	
ABILITIES	**Canticles of the Omnissiah** (see *Codex: Adeptus Mechanicus*) **Broad Spectrum Data-tether:** At the start of the Morale phase, until the end of the phase, add 1 to the Leadership characteristic of **<Forge World>** models from your army whilst their unit is within 3" of any friendly models with a broad spectrum data-tether.	**Hover Platform:** This model does not suffer the penalty for moving and firing Heavy weapons. **Explodes:** When this model is destroyed, roll one D6 before removing it from play. On a 6 it explodes, and each unit within 6" suffers D3 mortal wounds.
FACTION KEYWORDS	Imperium, Adeptus Mechanicus, Skitarii, <Forge World>	
KEYWORDS	Vehicle, Skorpius Disintegrator	

ARCHAEOPTER TRANSVECTOR

DAMAGE

Some of this model's characteristics change as it suffers damage, as shown below:

REMAINING W	M	BS	A
6-10+	20-50"	3+	3
3-5	20-35"	4+	D3
1-2	20-25"	5+	1

NAME	M	WS	BS	S	T	W	A	Ld	Sv
Archaeopter Transvector	*	5+	*	6	7	10	*	9	3+

An Archaeopter Transvector is a single model equipped with: 2 cognis heavy stubbers; twin cognis heavy stubber. It has a command uplink.

WEAPON	RANGE	TYPE	S	AP	D	ABILITIES
Cognis heavy stubber	36"	Heavy 3	4	0	1	You can choose this weapon to shoot with even if the bearer Advanced. When resolving an attack made with this weapon, if the bearer Advanced, subtract 2 from the hit roll.
Twin cognis heavy stubber	36"	Heavy 6	4	0	1	You can choose this weapon to shoot with even if the bearer Advanced. When resolving an attack made with this weapon, if the bearer Advanced, subtract 2 from the hit roll.

WARGEAR OPTIONS	• This model can have a chaff launcher instead of a command uplink.

ABILITIES	**Canticles of the Omnissiah** (see *Codex: Adeptus Mechanicus*) **Command Uplink:** If this model has a command uplink, friendly <**Forge World**> units can use this model's Leadership instead of their own whilst they are within 6" of this model. **Chaff Launcher:** When resolving an attack made with a ranged weapon against a model with a chaff launcher, reduce the Damage characteristic of that weapon by 1, to a minimum of 1, for that attack. **Manoeuvrable Craft:** When this model moves in your Movement phase, first pivot it on the spot up to 90° (this does not contribute to how far the model moves), then move the model straight forwards. It can pivot up to 90° one more time, at any point, during this move. When this model Advances, add 20" to its Move characteristic until the end of the Movement phase instead of making an Advance roll.	**Airborne:** You cannot charge with this unit, and this unit can only be chosen as a target of a charge if the unit making the charge can **Fly**. You can only fight with this unit if it is within 1" of any enemy units that can **Fly**, and this unit can only make close combat attacks against units that can **Fly**. Enemy units can only make close combat attacks against this unit if they can **Fly**. **Explodes:** When this model is destroyed, roll one D6 before any embarked models disembark, and before removing it from play. On a 6 it explodes, and each unit within 6" suffers D3 mortal wounds. **Hover Jet:** Before this model moves in your Movement phase, you can declare it will hover. Its Move characteristic becomes 20" until the end of the phase, and it loses the Airborne, Hard to Hit and Manoeuvrable Craft abilities until the beginning of your next Movement phase. **Hard to Hit:** When resolving an attack made with a ranged weapon against this model, subtract 1 from the hit roll.

TRANSPORT	This model has a transport capacity of 6 **Secutarii**, <**Forge World**> **Electro-Priests**, <**Forge World**> **Tech-Priest** or <**Forge World**> **Skitarii Infantry** models. It cannot transport **Belisarius Cawl**.
FACTION KEYWORDS	**Imperium, Adeptus Mechanicus,** <**Forge World**>
KEYWORDS	**Vehicle, Aircraft, Transport, Fly, Archaeopter, Archaeopter Transvector**

ARCHAEOPTER STRATORAPTOR

DAMAGE
Some of this model's characteristics change as it suffers damage, as shown below:

REMAINING W	M	BS	A
6-10+	20-50"	3+	3
3-5	20-35"	4+	D3
1-2	20-25"	5+	1

NAME	M	WS	BS	S	T	W	A	Ld	Sv
Archaeopter Stratoraptor	*	5+	*	6	7	10	*	9	3+

An Archaeopter Stratoraptor is a single model equipped with: 2 cognis heavy stubbers; 2 heavy phosphor blasters; twin cognis lascannon. It has a command uplink.

WEAPON	RANGE	TYPE	S	AP	D	ABILITIES
Cognis heavy stubber	36"	Heavy 3	4	0	1	You can choose this weapon to shoot with even if the bearer Advanced. When resolving an attack made with this weapon, if the bearer Advanced, subtract 2 from the hit roll.
Heavy phosphor blaster	36"	Heavy 3	6	-2	1	When resolving an attack made with this weapon, the target does not receive the benefit of cover.
Twin cognis lascannon	48"	Heavy 2	9	-3	D6	You can choose this weapon to shoot with even if the bearer Advanced. When resolving an attack made with this weapon, if the bearer Advanced, subtract 2 from the hit roll.

WARGEAR OPTIONS	• This model can have a chaff launcher instead of a command uplink.

ABILITIES	**Canticles of the Omnissiah** (see *Codex: Adeptus Mechanicus*) **Command Uplink:** If this model has a command uplink, friendly <Forge World> units can use this model's Leadership instead of their own whilst they are within 6" of this model. **Chaff Launcher:** When resolving an attack made with a ranged weapon against a model with a chaff launcher, reduce the Damage characteristic of that weapon by 1, to a minimum of 1, for that attack. **Manoeuvrable Craft:** When this model moves in your Movement phase, first pivot it on the spot up to 90° (this does not contribute to how far the model moves), then move the model straight forwards. It can pivot up to 90° one more time, at any point, during this move. When this model Advances, add 20" to its Move characteristic until the end of the Movement phase instead of making an Advance roll.	**Airborne:** You cannot charge with this unit, and this unit can only be chosen as a target of a charge if the unit making the charge can FLY. You can only fight with this unit if it is within 1" of any enemy units that can FLY, and this unit can only make close combat attacks against units that can FLY. Enemy units can only make close combat attacks against this unit if they can FLY. **Explodes:** When this model is destroyed, roll one D6 before removing it from play. On a 6 it explodes, and each unit within 6" suffers D3 mortal wounds. **Hover Jet:** Before this model moves in your Movement phase, you can declare it will hover. Its Move characteristic becomes 20" until the end of the phase, and it loses the Airborne, Hard to Hit and Manoeuvrable Craft abilities until the beginning of your next Movement phase. **Hard to Hit:** When resolving an attack made with a ranged weapon against this model, subtract 1 from the hit roll.

FACTION KEYWORDS	IMPERIUM, ADEPTUS MECHANICUS, <FORGE WORLD>
KEYWORDS	VEHICLE, AIRCRAFT, FLY, ARCHAEOPTER, ARCHAEOPTER STRATORAPTOR

ARCHAEOPTER FUSILAVE

NAME	M	WS	BS	S	T	W	A	Ld	Sv
Archaeopter Fusilave	*	5+	*	6	7	10	*	9	3+

An Archaeopter Fusilave is a single model equipped with: 4 cognis heavy stubbers. It has a command uplink.

DAMAGE

Some of this model's characteristics change as it suffers damage, as shown below:

REMAINING W	M	BS	A
6-10+	20-50"	3+	3
3-5	20-35"	4+	D3
1-2	20-25"	5+	1

WEAPON	RANGE	TYPE	S	AP	D	ABILITIES
Cognis heavy stubber	36"	Heavy 3	4	0	1	You can choose this weapon to shoot with even if the bearer Advanced. When resolving an attack made with this weapon, if the bearer Advanced, subtract 2 from the hit roll.

WARGEAR OPTIONS	• This model can have a chaff launcher instead of a command uplink.

ABILITIES	

Canticles of the Omnissiah (see *Codex: Adeptus Mechanicus*)

Bomb Rack: At the end of your Movement phase, this model can drop heavy bombs on one enemy unit it moved over in that phase. To a maximum of ten D6, roll three D6 for each **Vehicle** and **Monster** model in that unit and one D6 for each other model in that unit. For each roll of 4+ that unit suffers 1 mortal wound.

Command Uplink: If this model has a command uplink, friendly **<Forge World>** units can use this model's Leadership instead of their own whilst they are within 6" of this model.

Chaff Launcher: When resolving an attack made with a ranged weapon against a model with a chaff launcher, reduce the Damage characteristic of that weapon by 1, to a minimum of 1, for that attack.

Manoeuvrable Craft: When this model moves in your Movement phase, first pivot it on the spot up to 90° (this does not contribute to how far the model moves), then move the model straight forwards. It can pivot up to 90° one more time, at any point, during this move. When this model Advances, add 20" to its Move characteristic until the end of the Movement phase instead of making an Advance roll.

Hard to Hit: When resolving an attack made with a ranged weapon against this model, subtract 1 from the hit roll.

Airborne: You cannot charge with this unit, and this unit can only be chosen as a target of a charge if the unit making the charge can **Fly**. You can only fight with this unit if it is within 1" of any enemy units that can **Fly**, and this unit can only make close combat attacks against units that can **Fly**. Enemy units can only make close combat attacks against this unit if they can **Fly**.

Explodes: When this model is destroyed, roll one D6 before removing it from play. On a 6 it explodes, and each unit within 6" suffers D3 mortal wounds.

Hover Jet: Before this model moves in your Movement phase, you can declare it will hover. Its Move characteristic becomes 20" until the end of the phase, and it loses the Airborne, Hard to Hit and Manoeuvrable Craft abilities until the beginning of your next Movement phase.

FACTION KEYWORDS	**Imperium, Adeptus Mechanicus, <Forge World>**
KEYWORDS	**Vehicle, Aircraft, Fly, Archaeopter, Archaeopter Fusilave**

POINTS VALUES

If you are playing a matched play game, or a game that uses a points limit, you can use the following lists to determine the total points cost of your army. To do so, simply add together the points costs of all your models and their wargear.

UNITS

UNIT	MODELS PER UNIT	POINTS PER MODEL (Not including wargear)
Archaeopter Fusilave	1	102
Archaeopter Stratoraptor	1	70
Archaeopter Transvector	1	92
Pteraxii Skystalkers	5-10	15
Pteraxii Sterylizors	5-10	17
Serberys Raiders	3-9	14
Serberys Sulphurhounds	3-9	16
Skorpius Disintegrator	1	85
Skorpius Dunerider	1	65
Tech-Priest Manipulus	1	65

WARGEAR

ITEM	POINTS PER ITEM
Broad spectrum data-tether	0
Chaff launcher	20
Command uplink	0
Enhanced data-tether	5

MELEE WEAPONS

WEAPON	POINTS PER WEAPON
Cavalry sabre	0
Clawed limbs	0
Mechadendrites	0
Omnissian staff	0
Power maul	4
Pteraxii talons	0
Taser goad	4

RANGED WEAPONS

WEAPON	POINTS PER WEAPON
Archeo-revolver	2
Belleros energy cannon	20
Cognis heavy stubber	2
Disruptor missile launcher	0
Ferrumite cannon	25
Flechette blaster	0
Flechette carbine	0
Galvanic carbine	0
Heavy phosphor blaster	0
Magnarail lance	0
Phosphor blast carbine	15
Phosphor blast pistol	5
Phosphor pistol	1
Phosphor torch	0
Sulphur breath	0
Transonic cannon	0
Twin cognis heavy stubber	4
Twin cognis lascannon	40

COHORTS OF THE FORGE WORLDS

While the priesthood and cybernetic warriors of many forge worlds religiously maintain the red of Mars upon their robes and armour panels as a sign of fealty – even if merely ceremonial – the accoutrements of the Machine God's devotees are as varied in hue and form as the titles claimed by its zealous Tech-Priests.

Serberys Sulphurhound with phosphor blast carbine

Serberys Raider with galvanic carbine

Rounding a bulkhead in their ship's vast enginarium, Serberys cavalry smash aside the filth-encrusted Daemons converging on the outer Geller field fortress vault. Sulphurhounds incinerate the cloud of buzzing flies, while Raiders shatter the foul creatures' skulls with expert shots.

Magnarail lance

Pteraxii Sterylizor with phosphor torch

Tech-Priest Manipulus with transonic cannon

Thrumming smoothly over the war-torn and tectonically active terrain, Skorpius Disintegrators train their augurs on distant targets while Skorpius Duneriders rapidly deliver squads of Skitarii to the front lines.

HOLY ORDER WARLORD TRAITS

The intricate web of shifting religious, political, technological and philosophical leanings within the Adeptus Mechanicus is bewildering to those outside the priesthood. Yet even as sub-cults, movements and schisms are in constant flux, four Holy Orders are commonly recognised on the majority of forge worlds.

If an **ADEPTUS MECHANICUS CHARACTER** model (excluding named characters) is your Warlord, you can select a Warlord Trait from below for them instead of using the Warlord Traits table from *Codex: Adeptus Mechanicus*.

LEARNINGS OF THE GENETOR

Genetors probe the mysteries of the biological. Molecular striation, cyborg interfaces, genetic manipulation and alchemical behavioural modification are all avenues of interest to those determined to master the boundaries of the flesh.

At the start of your turn, you can select one of the aura abilities below. Until the start of your next turn, this Warlord is treated as having that aura ability on their datasheet.

- **Hyper-cybernetic Physiology:** Roll one D6 each time a friendly **<FORGE WORLD> KATAPHRON BREACHER**, **<FORGE WORLD> KATAPHRON DESTROYER** or **<FORGE WORLD> SERVITOR** model would lose a wound whilst within 6" of this Warlord; on a 5+, that wound is not lost.

- **Biochemical Aggression:** When resolving an attack made with a melee weapon by a friendly **<FORGE WORLD>** model whilst its unit is within 6" of this Warlord, on an unmodified wound roll of 6 improve the Armour Penetration characteristic of that weapon by 2 for that attack (e.g. AP 0 becomes AP -2).

- **Excoriated Fear-Responses:** When a Morale test is taken for a friendly **<FORGE WORLD>** unit within 6" of this Warlord, do not roll the dice; it is automatically passed.

ANALYSES OF THE LOGOS

Data-vores and biocogitators, logi amass huge stores of information, analysing data from thousands of sources at once until they can rationalise every move the enemy make, their levels of prediction bordering on prophetic.

At the start of your turn, you can select one of the aura abilities below. Until the start of your next turn, this Warlord is treated as having that aura ability on their datasheet.

- **Predicted Movements:** When resolving an Overwatch attack made by a model in a friendly **<FORGE WORLD> INFANTRY** unit within 6" of this Warlord, a hit roll of 5 or 6 scores a hit.

- **Empyric Prognosis:** Roll one D6 when a friendly **<FORGE WORLD>** model would lose a wound as a result of a mortal wound in the Psychic phase whilst its unit is within 6" of this Warlord; on a 4+ that wound is not lost.

- **Flaws of the Foe:** When resolving an attack made with a ranged weapon by a friendly **<FORGE WORLD>** model within 6" of this Warlord, on an unmodified hit roll of 6 the Armour Penetration characteristic of that weapon is improved by 1 for that attack (e.g. AP 0 becomes AP -1).

01010100 01101000 01100101 00100000 01010100 01100101 01100101 01110100
01101000 00100000 01101111 01100110 00100000 01110100 01101000 01100101
00100000 01000011 01101111 01100111 00100000 01101011 01101110 01101111
01110111 00100000 01100001 01101100 01101100

The opening data-packet of the Versus Primaris, illuminated binharic cant broadcast from Holy Mars and emblazoned across the sensorium of the Faithful. For the benefit of those yet to receive the blessing of noospheric augmentation, the Low Gothic translation to 'All Will Praise the Omnissiah', lacks the algorithmical beauty of the original.

DIVINATIONS OF THE MAGOS

Magi are masters of fiercely guarded knowledge, pursuing esoteric agendas to enhance their specialisms at all costs. No risk is too great and no gambit too unwise in their ceaseless and predatory acquisition of ancient lore.

At the start of your turn, you can select one of the aura abilities below. Until the start of your next turn, this Warlord is treated as having that aura ability on their datasheet.

- **Overloaded Safeguards:** When resolving an attack made with a ranged weapon by a friendly <Forge World> model within 6" of this Warlord, an unmodified hit roll of 6 scores 1 additional hit.

- **Aggressive Subroutines:** You can re-roll charge rolls made for friendly <Forge World> units whilst they are within 6" of this Warlord.

- **Predatory Programming:** When a friendly <Forge World> unit within 6" of this Warlord Advances, roll one additional D6 and discard one of the dice when making the Advance roll.

FABRICATIONS OF THE ARTISAN

Artisans of the Adeptus Mechanicus create wondrous artefacts of war, installing circuits of such beauty or capacitor-nodes of such fine calibration that their machine spirits respond with divine gratitude.

At the start of your turn, you can select one of the aura abilities below. Until the start of your next turn, this Warlord is treated as having that aura ability on their datasheet.

- **Exquisite Calibrations:** When resolving an attack made with a ranged weapon by a friendly <Forge World> model within 6" of this Warlord against a unit that is within half range, improve the Armour Penetration characteristic of that weapon by 1 for that attack (e.g. AP 0 becomes AP -1).

- **Mastery of the Motive Force:** When resolving an attack made with an arc weapon by a friendly <Forge World> model within 6" of this Warlord against a Vehicle unit, an unmodified wound roll of 6 inflicts 1 mortal wound on the target in addition to any other damage.

- **Enhanced Engine Interfaces:** Friendly Vehicle models within 6" of this Warlord can shoot in a turn in which they Fell Back.

ADEPTUS MECHANICUS STRATAGEMS

If your army is Battle-forged and includes any ADEPTUS MECHANICUS Detachments (excluding Auxiliary Support Detachments), you have access to the Stratagems shown here, and can spend Command Points to activate them. These reflect the unique strategies used by the Adeptus Mechanicus on the battlefield.

OLFACTORUM AGGRESSOR IMPERATIVE
1CP

Adeptus Mechanicus Stratagem

Once inloaded, the imperative hypersensitises detection capacity, linking it directly with any aggression protocols.

Use this Stratagem in your Movement phase. Select one SERBERYS SULPHURHOUNDS unit from your army. Until the end of the phase, when that unit Advances, add 6" to its Move characteristic instead of making an Advance roll. In addition, until the end of the turn, models in that unit shoot as if they did not move that turn.

RAPTORIAL STRAFING FIRE
1CP

Adeptus Mechanicus Stratagem

Roused to ire, the Stratoraptor's machine spirit punishes the crawling enemy beneath it.

Use this Stratagem in your Shooting phase when an ARCHAEOPTER STRATORAPTOR model from your army is chosen to shoot with. Until the end of the phase, when resolving an attack made by that model against a unit that cannot FLY, add 1 to the hit roll.

STEELRAIN FUSILLADE
1CP

Adeptus Mechanicus Stratagem

Unleashing a storm of needle-like projectiles, Skystalkers keep their enemy suppressed with unceasing hails of fire.

Use this Stratagem in your Shooting phase when a PTERAXII SKYSTALKERS unit from your army is chosen to shoot with. Select one enemy unit that is not TITANIC. Until the end of the phase, when resolving an attack made by a model in that Pteraxii Skystalkers unit against the selected unit, if a hit is scored the target is suppressed until the start of your next turn. When resolving an attack made with a ranged weapon by a model in a suppressed unit, subtract 1 from the hit roll.

TACTICA OBLIQUA
2CP

Adeptus Mechanicus Stratagem

Cogitating several steps ahead, the Serberys Raiders obey a sudden protocol change, pulling them out of reach and leaving a rash enemy exposed.

Use this Stratagem in your opponent's Charge phase when a SERBERYS RAIDERS unit from your army is chosen as the target of a charge for the first time that turn. Instead of firing Overwatch, that unit can move or Fall Back as if it were your Movement phase (it cannot Advance as part of this move).

SEISMIC BOMB
1CP

Adeptus Mechanicus Stratagem

Driven into the strata by powerful rockets, seismic bombs erupt in savage vibrations that throw warriors from their feet and disrupt drive units.

Use this Stratagem in your Movement phase after moving an ARCHAEOPTER FUSILAVE unit from your army. Select one enemy unit that ARCHAEOPTER FUSILAVE unit moved over that phase. That enemy unit is shaken in your opponent's next Movement phase. If a unit that cannot FLY and is not TITANIC is shaken, halve its Move characteristic and the result of any Advance and charge rolls made for it.

DEEPLY SUNK TALONS
1CP

Adeptus Mechanicus Stratagem

Caught upon the talons of hunters whose reasoning has been pared back to finely tuned instincts, escape for those they catch is unlikely.

Use this Stratagem in your opponent's Movement phase, when an enemy INFANTRY unit within 1" of any PTERAXII STERYLIZORS units from your army is chosen to Fall Back. Roll one D6; on a 2+, that enemy unit cannot Fall Back this turn.

STEREOSCOPIC TRIANGULATION

1CP

Adeptus Mechanicus Stratagem

Meshing the Disintegrator's threat augurs, servo-scryers and spectranima onto a single target spells its doom.

Use this Stratagem in your Shooting phase when a **Skorpius Disintegrator** model from your army is chosen to shoot with. Until the end of the phase, if that model shoots all of the weapons it is equipped with at the same target, then, when resolving an attack made by that model, add 1 to the hit roll and the target does not receive the benefit of cover.

CIRCUITOUS ASSASSINS

1CP

Adeptus Mechanicus Stratagem

Ruststalker hunting imperatives see them swiftly and silently encircle the foe, the hum of their blades stilled.

Use this Stratagem at the start of your Movement phase. Select one **Sicarian Ruststalkers** unit from your army that is wholly within 9" of any battlefield edge. Remove that unit from the battlefield. At the end of that Movement phase, you can set up that unit anywhere on the battlefield that is more than 9" from any enemy units and wholly within 9" of any battlefield edge.

EVACUATION SEQUENCE

0CP

Adeptus Mechanicus Stratagem

Sufficiently sanctified, a Dunerider's machine spirit will do everything in its power to save its cargo.

Use this Stratagem in any phase when a **Skorpius Dunerider** model from your army is destroyed, before any embarked units disembark. Until the end of the phase, when a model disembarks from that **Skorpius Dunerider** model, do not roll to see if it is slain.

PERPETUAL INCENSE

1CP

Adeptus Mechanicus Stratagem

In the press of combat, incense exhausts pump out a constant blinding fog, masking the Dragoons' forms.

Use this Stratagem at the start of the Fight phase. Select one **Sydonian Dragoons** unit from your army. Until the end of the phase, when resolving an attack made against that unit, subtract 1 from the hit roll.

ELECTROSTATIC OVERCHARGE

1CP

Adeptus Mechanicus Stratagem

By chanting fiery psalms in praise of the Motive Force, Corpuscarii inflame the potential of their generous gift.

Use this Stratagem in your Shooting phase when a **Corpuscarii Electro-Priests** unit from your army is chosen to shoot with. Until the end of the phase, electrostatic gauntlets models in that unit are equipped with have an Armour Penetration characteristic of -2.

MECHANICUS LOCUM

1CP

Adeptus Mechanicus Stratagem

Every congregation of Tech-Priests comprises masters of arcane knowledge, zealous leaders of man and machine.

Use this Stratagem before the battle, after nominating your Warlord. Select one **<Forge World> Character** model from your army that does not have a Warlord Trait and determine one Warlord Trait for it; it is regarded as your Warlord for the purposes of that Warlord Trait. Each Warlord Trait in your army must be unique (if randomly generated, re-roll duplicate results).

PATTERN ITERATION IDENTIFIED

1CP

Adeptus Mechanicus Stratagem

Once targets are identified by pattern iteration recognition, weak spots are quickly established.

Use this Stratagem in your Shooting phase when an **Ironstrider Ballistarii** unit from your army is chosen to shoot with. Until the end of the phase, when resolving an attack made by a model in that unit against a unit without the **Titanic** keyword, add 1 to the wound roll.

ELECTRO-FILAMENT COUNTERMEASURES

1CP

Adeptus Mechanicus Stratagem

A glittering cloud of nanofibres descends, its distorting and fracturing effect shutting down enemy comms.

Use this Stratagem at the end of your Movement phase. Select one **Archaeopter** unit equipped with a command uplink from your army. Until the start of your next turn, enemy models aura abilities have no effect whilst within 6" of that unit.

FORGE WORLD DOGMAS

The forge worlds of the Adeptus Mechanicus are parochial, occasionally isolationist and highly competitive. Layers of religious fealty and contracts of technological trade bind them together, yet many forge worlds have existed for tens of millennia, in that time diverging and developing far from the others.

Most forces of the Adeptus Mechanicus belong to a forge world. This is represented by the <**Forge World**> keyword, as described in *Codex: Adeptus Mechanicus*. If you have chosen a forge world that does not have a forge world dogma, or you have created your own forge world, the rules presented over the following pages allow you to create your own dogma for your forge world.

If your army is Battle-forged, all units with the <**Forge World**> keyword will receive a Forge World Dogma, so long as every other unit in their Detachment is from the same forge world. If your chosen forge world does not have an associated Dogma in *Codex: Adeptus Mechanicus*, you can create one by selecting one primary ability below, followed by one of its associated secondary abilities.

RAD-SATURATED FORGE WORLD

Whether as a result of natural phenomena, ancient internecine wars fought with apocalyptic weapons or calamitous accidents caused by lost knowledge, this forge world is heavily irradiated. When holy wars of requisition are unleashed, this planet's Tech-Priests and cybernetic maniples carry the curse of invisible excoriation with them.

PRIMARY: RADIANT DISCIPLES

When resolving an attack made with a ranged weapon against an **Infantry** unit with this dogma that is not within 12", subtract 1 from the Strength characteristic of that weapon for that attack.

SECONDARY: LUMINARY SUFFUSION

Replace the Rad-saturation ability of models with this dogma with the following ability:

'**Rad-saturation:** Subtract 1 from the Strength and Toughness characteristics of an enemy model whilst its unit is within 3" of any models from your army with this ability.'

SECONDARY: SCARIFYING WEAPONRY

Radium weapons models with this dogma are equipped with have an Armour Penetration characteristic of -1.

SECONDARY: OMNISSIAH'S SHIELD

When resolving an attack made with a melee weapon against an **Infantry** unit with this dogma, reduce the Armour Penetration characteristic of that weapon by 1 for that attack, to a minimum of 0 (e.g. AP -1 becomes AP 0).

SECONDARY: MACHINE GOD'S CHOSEN

When a Morale test is taken for a unit with this dogma, halve the number of models that flee (rounding up).

EXPANSIONIST FORGE WORLD

The Tech-Priests of this forge world are not content to labour in isolation. They are fiercely aggressive, funding large numbers of Explorator Fleets in their quest to uncover the hidden truths left by the Machine God. Always on the move, their armies are swift and manoeuvrable.

PRIMARY: ACCELERATED ACTUATORS

At the end of the Charge phase, if a unit with this dogma made a charge move, was charged or performed a Heroic Intervention, improve the Armour Penetration characteristic of melee weapons models in that unit are equipped with by 1 until the end of the turn (e.g. AP 0 becomes AP -1).

SECONDARY: FORWARD OPERATIONS

At the start of the first battle round, before the first turn begins, **Skitarii Rangers** units with this dogma can move up to 6". This unit must end that move more than 9" away from any enemy models. If both players have units that can do this, the player who is taking the first turn moves their units first.

SECONDARY: ACQUISITIVE REACH

Add 6" to the Range characteristic of Rapid Fire weapons models with this dogma are equipped with.

SECONDARY: RUGGED EXPLORATORS

Models with this dogma do not suffer the penalty for Advancing and firing Assault weapons.

Secondary: Dominus Command Net

Replace the Broad Spectrum Data-tether ability of models with this dogma with the following ability:

'**Broad Spectrum Data-tether:** Add 1 to the Leadership characteristic of friendly **<Forge World>** models whilst their unit is within 9" of any models that have a broad spectrum data-tether.'

DATA-HOARD FORGE WORLD

This forge world, whether it brazenly flaunts its superiority or hides it through fear of attack or censure, has hoarded its arcane knowledge until it has attained mastery in hundreds of areas of technological esoterica. Through caches of STC fragments, subversive theft from other forge worlds or even treating with xenos, this forge world's masters jealously clutch insights into ore refining, duralloy formulae, crystal-flex optics, exotic energies and all the mysteries of the mechanical, or so some claim.

Primary: Magnabonded Alloys

When a **Vehicle** model with this dogma would lose a wound, roll one D6; on a 6 that wound is not lost.

Secondary: Omnitrac Impellors

Add 1" to the Move characteristic of **Kataphron Breachers**, **Kataphron Destroyers** and **Onager Dunecrawler** models with this dogma.

Secondary: Servo-focused Auguries

When resolving an attack made with a cognis ranged weapon by a model with this dogma against a unit that is within half range, you can re-roll the hit roll.

Secondary: Autosavant Spirits

At the start of your turn, if a **Vehicle** model with this dogma has lost any wounds, it can regain up to 1 lost wound.

Secondary: Trans-node Power Cores

When resolving an attack made with an arc weapon by a model with this dogma, an unmodified hit roll of 5 or 6 scores 1 additional hit.

FORGE WORLD CANTICLES OF THE OMNISSIAH

All forge worlds zealously praise the Machine God and the others of the holy trinity: the Omnissiah and the Motive Force. Yet differing interpretations and violent schisms stain the history of the Adeptus Mechanicus like rust, resulting in no few wars. Today, many forge worlds retain religious idiosyncrasies.

Before the battle, if your Warlord is an **ADEPTUS MECHANICUS CHARACTER** and their **<FORGE WORLD>** is one of those listed below, you can select one of the Canticles in the Canticles of the Omnissiah table (see *Codex: Adeptus Mechanicus*) to be replaced by that **<FORGE WORLD>**'s Canticle below.

RYZA: CITATION IN SAVAGERY

Binharic exultations accompany the rending blows of Ryza's troops, a cybernetic chorus that venerates the Machine God and infuses them with zealous savagery.

The Armour Penetration characteristic of melee weapons models in the affected unit are equipped with is improved by 1 (e.g. AP 0 becomes AP -1).

MARS: PANEGYRIC PROCESSION

The Tech-Priests of the Red Planet lead their disciples in a cortege of war. The buzz of static psalms chanted in synchronicity unites all in the stately eradication of the heretic and blasphemer.

Models in affected units do not suffer the penalty for moving and firing Heavy weapons. Increase the Strength characteristic of Heavy weapons models in the affected unit are equipped with by 1.

LUCIUS: LUMINESCENT BLESSING

As the cohorts of Lucius recite their dazzling consecration, energy is redirected to infuse their masterwork alloys and even the lambent glow of protective fields ignites in a halo of divine defence.

Improve the invulnerable save of models in affected units by 1 (to a maximum of 4+).

METALICA: TRIBUTE OF EMPHATIC VENERATION

A cacophonous chorale pouring from the vox-grilles and emitters of Metalica's faithful venerates the Omnissiah with such deafening praise as to perturb their enemies.

When resolving an attack against an affected unit by an enemy model within 9", subtract 1 from the hit roll.

GRAIA: MANTRA OF DISCIPLINE

Doctrinal imperatives reinforce the steel-minded tenacity of Graia's warriors as their enemies near, turning charging foes into naught but data to be processed and deleted.

When resolving an Overwatch attack made by a model in an affected unit, a hit roll of 5 or 6 scores a hit.

AGRIPINAA: VERSE OF VENGEANCE

Rousing code in binharic duometer incites fury for the lost worlds around Agripinaa. In the grip of vengeance, the devoted extend their remaining functions for one last act of retribution.

When an **INFANTRY** or **CAVALRY** model in an affected unit is destroyed, roll one D6 before removing that model from play. On a 5+, that model can either shoot with one of its ranged weapons as if it were your Shooting phase or make one attack with one of its melee weapons as if it were the Fight phase.

STYGIES: PLEA OF THE VEILED HUNTER

In silent supplication to the Machine God, a concentrated burst of noospheric negation manifests as a heavy band of shadow, allowing the warriors of Stygies to disengage seamlessly from their foe and instantly strike back.

Affected units can shoot in a turn in which they Fell Back, but if a unit does so, when resolving an attack made with a ranged weapon by a model in that unit that turn, subtract 1 from the hit roll.

ADEPTUS MECHANICUS NAME GENERATOR

If you wish to randomly generate a name for your logic-driven Adeptus Mechanicus zealots, you can roll a D66 and consult the tables below. To roll a D66, simply roll two D6, one after the other – the first represents tens, and the second represents digits, giving you a result between 11 and 66.

D66	ALPHA ELEMENT	D66	BETA ELEMENT
11	Sy-gex	11	-XXVII
12	Lho	12	Mojaro
13	Tyr	13	Tov
14	Teppa-Nyxos	14	-6e20F
15	Dak	15	Vladimus
16	Kor	16	Knoch
21	Ar	21	Thannek
22	Dox	22	Malavont
23	Kappic-Schoelendt	23	-089
24	Sek	24	/323Mk12
25	Tyba	25	-998/56c
26	Protos-Reductus	26	Virellan
31	Dorox	31	-1111
32	09	32	Drax
33	Alb	33	Xixos
34	Bartolomus	34	Gedd-38f
35	Garba	35	Dol
36	Mu	36	Osmium
41	8-	41	-511
42	Rhy	42	-888.88
43	Thusdorius	43	-66.75/Mk98
44	Dos	44	Ω5-Decarote
45	Augreus	45	-666/2
46	Exitor-Dho	46	-802
51	Delpha	51	-79.09/5
52	Fel	52	Ondos
53	Chu	53	-1010
54	Actus	54	-18.1
55	Vettius	55	Kroll
56	Xor	56	Yaekobus-Δ
61	Neng-Pho	61	Eng
62	Decima	62	Rhombor
63	Bheta	63	-1/5
64	Vitruvius	64	Telok
65	Zhu	65	-0.44/K
66	Gregorius	66	Veriliad

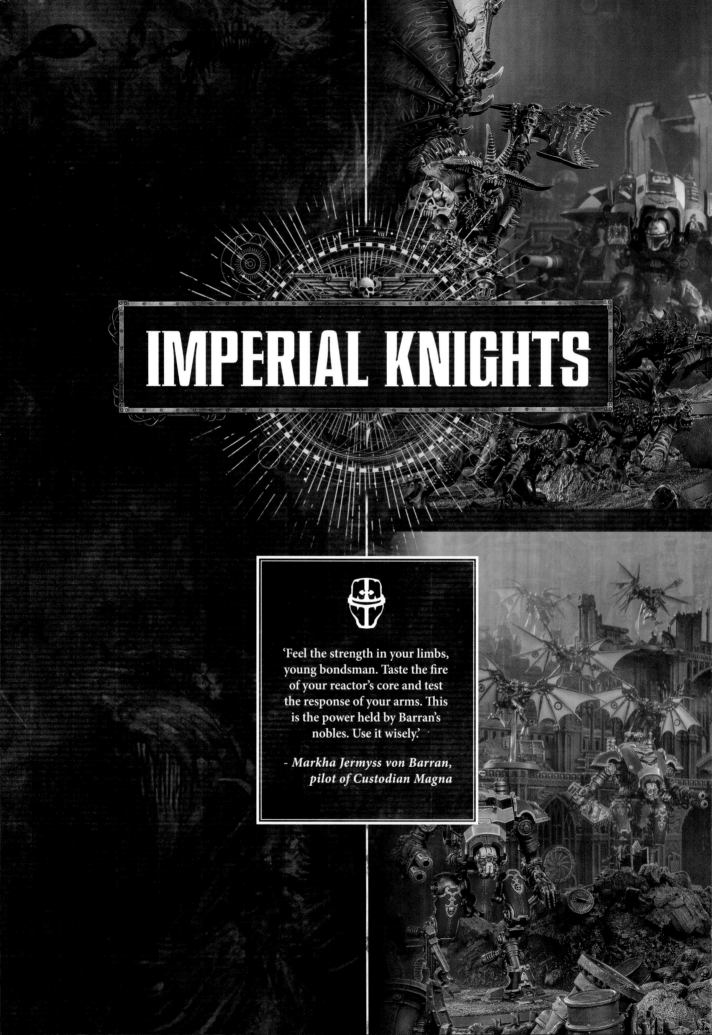

IMPERIAL KNIGHTS

'Feel the strength in your limbs, young bondsman. Taste the fire of your reactor's core and test the response of your arms. This is the power held by Barran's nobles. Use it wisely.'

- *Markha Jermyss von Barran,*
pilot of Custodian Magna

THE STRIKE OF THE LANCE

The rules in this section supplement those found in *Codex: Imperial Knights* and can be used in any open play, narrative play or matched play game. They include new rules for <Questor Allegiance> Detachments, Warlord Traits, Stratagems and rules for creating your own Household Tradition.

Name Generator

Opposite you will find a useful tool to help you forge names for the Knights of your household, and the brave Nobles who pilot them.

Stratagems

If your army is Battle-forged and includes any **IMPERIAL KNIGHTS** Detachments, the Stratagems on pages 58-59 can be used in addition to those presented in *Codex: Imperial Knights*.

Household Traditions

With the exception of Freeblades, all Imperial Knights belong to a household. This is represented by the <**HOUSEHOLD**> keyword. If you have chosen an Imperial Knights household that does not have a Household Tradition, or you have created your own Imperial Knights household, the rules presented on pages 60-61 allow you to create your own Household Tradition for your Imperial Knights household. This allows you to personalise your Imperial Knights and represent the myriad of cultures, fighting styles and values associated with different households.

Questor Allegiance Oaths

Imperial Knights owe their allegiance to either the Imperium of Man or the Machine Cult of the Adeptus Mechanicus. This is represented by the <**QUESTOR ALLEGIANCE**> keyword. The rules presented on page 62 are new rules for Imperial Knights based on their choice of allegiance, be it the gallant and exalted Imperial Knights of the Questor Imperialis allegiance, or the logical and efficient Imperial Knights of the Questor Mechanicus allegiance.

Warlord Traits

If an **IMPERIAL KNIGHTS CHARACTER** model is your Warlord, you can generate a Warlord Trait from page 63 instead of generating one from another publication.

'Shipmaster, take the Padah March away from this filthy world. My Nobles, we have suffered greatly, but my conviction is greater still. Soon, we will have the means to cleanse far more than a single world of sorcery. Our guest has much more to divulge, of that I am certain.'

- Baroness Sordhen of House Terryn

IMPERIAL KNIGHTS NAME GENERATOR

The Nobles who pilot Imperial Knight suits usually belong to a household, and will share that household's family name. Many households use the titles sir and lady to honour those who pilot Knight suits, while others have their own traditions, using sair, markh, rit and countless others. Some use elements such as Von, Ap or Tan to denote a noble is 'of' a particular household, such as Luk Tan Chimaeros. If you wish to randomly generate a personal name for your nobles and a name for their Knight suit, you can roll a D66 and consult the tables below. To roll a D66, simply roll two D6, one after the other – the first represents tens, and the second represents digits, giving you a result between 11 and 66.

D66	NOBLE'S NAME		D66	KNIGHT SUIT'S NAME
11	Terenicia		11	Iron God
12	Luc		12	War Strider
13	Melandra		13	Retributor
14	Danial		14	Pride of Charadon
15	Hester		15	Adamant Wrath
16	Massimo		16	Unyielding Iron
21	Saris		21	Fury of Thaemar
22	Taurus		22	Impenetrable
23	Natanya		23	Carnivore
24	Griegor		24	Tempered Fury
25	Luxious		25	Honour Intractable
26	Maximilian		26	Hammerblow
31	Karyx		31	Intolerant
32	Selwyn		32	Glory Unblemished
33	Kalena		33	Ever-Stalwart
34	Brutus		34	Triumphal
35	Mairi		35	Honoured Vigilance
36	Darius		36	Unalloyed Victory
41	Olwyn		41	Bloody Broadsword
42	Seuitonius		42	Gilded Conqueror
43	Sordhen		43	The Beast Killer
44	Tybalt		44	Red Jackal
45	Gawenne		45	Coward's Bane
46	Mercutane		46	Blade of Justice
51	Joscelin		51	Hound Sinistor
52	Balthazar		52	Devastation Unbridled
53	Idae		53	Bane of Iron
54	Alarbus		54	Serpent's Bane
55	Ahrda		55	Oathkeeper
56	Guillam		56	Hate's Requiem
61	Goedhilde		61	Headsman
62	Baelkom		62	Redemption of Adamant
63	Izarael		63	Forsworn Wrath
64	Orlando		64	Manifest Vengeance
65	Irmaa		65	Black Heart
66	Edmane		66	Ferrum Magnificat

IMPERIAL KNIGHTS STRATAGEMS

If your army is Battle-forged and includes any IMPERIAL KNIGHTS Detachments, you have access to the Stratagems shown below, meaning you can spend Command Points to activate them. These help to reflect the unique tactics and strategies used by the Imperial Knights on the battlefield.

1CP

CLOSE-QUARTERS DESTRUCTION
Imperial Knights Stratagem
Knights Errant are lethal close-range killers, skilled at ensuring the enemy's utter annihilation.

Use this Stratagem in your Shooting phase, when a **KNIGHT ERRANT** model from your army is chosen to shoot with. Until the end of the phase, when resolving an attack made with a ranged weapon by that model against a unit that is within half the weapon's maximum range, you can re-roll the wound roll.

1CP

FLANKING MANOEUVRE
Imperial Knights Stratagem
The Knight focuses on swiftly redeploying mid-battle, its titanic stride eating up the distance as it flanks the foe.

Use this Stratagem in your Movement phase, when an **IMPERIAL KNIGHTS** model from your army is chosen to Advance. Add 8" to the model's Move characteristic until the end of the phase instead of making an Advance roll. That model must end the move within 12" of a battlefield edge, and cannot charge this turn.

1CP

THIN THEIR RANKS
Imperial Knights Stratagem
Not even the largest horde can long survive the fusillade of bondsworn young Nobles.

Use this Stratagem in your Shooting phase, when an **ARMIGER HELVERIN** model from your army is chosen to shoot with. Until the end of the phase, armiger autocannons that model is equipped with make 6 attacks when targeting a unit that contains 6 or more models, rather than 2D3.

1CP

CAPACITOR CHARGE
Imperial Knights Stratagem
With soothing prayers whispered to its machine spirit, the Noble coaxes the las-impulsor to unleash its fury.

Use this Stratagem in your Shooting phase, when a **KNIGHT PRECEPTOR** model from your army is chosen to shoot with. Until the end of the phase, change the Type characteristic of the high intensity profile of the las-impulsor that model is equipped with to Heavy 6.

1CP

HURLED WRECKAGE
Imperial Knights Stratagem
Spying another brutish silhouette, the Noble unerringly hurls the remains of their Knight's victim towards it.

Use this Stratagem when an enemy **VEHICLE** or **MONSTER** model is destroyed as a result of an attack made with a thunderstrike gauntlet, Freedom's Hand or the Paragon Gauntlet by an **IMPERIAL KNIGHTS** model from your army. When resolving that weapon's ability as a result of that enemy model being destroyed, if an enemy **VEHICLE** or **MONSTER** unit is selected as the target of the weapon's ability, that unit automatically suffers 3 mortal wounds – do not roll a dice.

1CP

PACK TACTICS
Imperial Knights Stratagem
Hunting in teams, the Nobles who pilot Armiger Warglaives attack as one, rending apart their prey.

Use this Stratagem in the Fight phase, when an **ARMIGER WARGLAIVE** model from your army is chosen to fight with. Select one enemy unit within 1" of that model. Until the end of the phase, increase the Attacks characteristic of that **ARMIGER WARGLAIVE** model, and all other friendly **ARMIGER WARGLAIVE** models within 1" of that enemy unit, by 1 for each other friendly **ARMIGER WARGLAIVE** model within 1" of that enemy unit (to a maximum of 2 additional attacks).

TROPHY CLAIM
1CP

Imperial Knights Stratagem

Taking down its monstrous foe, the Knight's emitters blare its triumph, invigorated by the kill.

Use this Stratagem when an enemy **TITANIC** model is destroyed as a result of an attack made with a melee weapon by an **IMPERIAL KNIGHTS** model from your army. Until the end of the battle, add 1 to the Attacks characteristic of that **IMPERIAL KNIGHTS** model.

SIEGEBREAKER BOMBARDMENT
1CP

Imperial Knights Stratagem

Overriding the servitor sub-arrays, the Castellan's Noble unleashes a cataclysmic shelling, resulting in utter ruin.

Use this Stratagem in your Shooting phase, when a **KNIGHT CASTELLAN** model from your army is chosen to shoot with. Until the end of the phase, so long as that model did not move in your previous Movement phase, add 1 to wound rolls for attacks made with twin siegebreaker cannons by that model.

ELECTROTHAUMIC OVERLOAD
2CP

Imperial Knights Stratagem

As the harpoon's generator is dangerously overcharged, vengeful electrogheists roar as they surge outwards.

Use this Stratagem in your Shooting phase, after inflicting any damage as a result of an attack made with a thundercoil harpoon by a **KNIGHT VALIANT** model from your army. Each enemy unit within 3" of the target of that attack suffers D3 mortal wounds.

LINEBREAKER
1CP

Imperial Knights Stratagem

Aggressively pushing through the swirl of melee, piles of dead in its wake, nothing can stop the Knight's advance.

Use this Stratagem in the Fight phase, when a **KNIGHT GALLANT** model from your army is chosen to fight with. Until the end of the phase, when making pile-in and consolidation moves, that model can move up to 6" instead of 3".

REPULSING CONFLAGRATION
1CP

Imperial Knights Stratagem

A blistering heat barrier and concussive cannonades drive back even determined enemies.

Use this Stratagem in your opponent's Charge phase, after a **KNIGHT VALIANT** model from your army has fired Overwatch. Until the end of the turn, subtract 2 from charge rolls made for units that target that model with a charge.

COVER THE ADVANCE
1CP

Imperial Knights Stratagem

The Knight Crusader unleashes a repressive barrage of firepower that cows the enemy before their power.

Use this Stratagem in your Shooting phase, after an enemy model has lost any wounds as the result of an attack made with a rapid-fire battle cannon, avenger gatling cannon or thermal cannon by a **KNIGHT CRUSADER** model from your army. Until the end of the turn, that enemy model's unit cannot fire Overwatch.

BELLIGERENT MACHINE SPIRIT
1CP

Imperial Knights Stratagem

Knight Wardens are prone to sudden acts of impulsive pugnacity, unloading a ferocious rate of fire at anyone threatening their lines.

Use this Stratagem in your Shooting phase, when a **KNIGHT WARDEN** model from your army is chosen to shoot with. Until the end of the phase, the range of that model's avenger gatling cannon is changed to 8" and when resolving an attack made with it, do not make a hit roll: it automatically scores a hit.

THUNDERSTRUCK
1CP

Imperial Knights Stratagem

With a roar like the clash of rival sky gods, the Knight Paladin's cannon erupts in a lightning salvo of death.

Use this Stratagem in your Shooting phase, when a **KNIGHT PALADIN** model from your army is chosen to shoot with. Until the end of the phase, the Damage characteristic of that model's rapid-fire battle cannon or Thunder of Voltoris is 3.

HOUSEHOLD TRADITIONS

Knightly households are ancient institutions, with martial traditions that stretch back for millennia. They are fiercely proud and individual, with rivalry and competition fierce among households sharing the same planet. Whether moulded by their environment, their glorious heroes or arduous necessity, no two are quite the same.

With the exception of Freeblades, all Imperial Knights belong to a household. This is represented by the <Household> keyword as described in *Codex: Imperial Knights*. If you have chosen an Imperial Knights household that does not have a Household Tradition, or you have created your own Imperial Knights household, the rules presented over the following pages allow you to create your own Household Tradition for your Imperial Knights household.

If your army is Battle-forged, all units in an **Imperial Knights** Super-heavy Detachment (other than **Freeblade** units) must be from the same household, but they will gain a Household Tradition (with the exception of **Freeblade** units). If your chosen household does not have an associated Household Tradition in *Codex: Imperial Knights*, you can create one by selecting two abilities from the list presented here.

Note that these rules are available to both **Questor Imperialis** and **Questor Mechanicus** households, and the usual rules for Household Traditions still apply with the following additions:

- All units in an **Imperial Knights** Super-heavy Detachment (other than **Freeblade** units) must have the same <Questor Allegiance>.
- Any rules marked with an asterisk (*) count as two selections.

Aggressive Persecution
The Nobles of this household are unstinting in ensuring that, when their foes go down, they stay down.

When a model with this tradition fires Overwatch or is chosen to shoot or fight with, you can re-roll a single dice when determining damage as a result of those attacks.

Blessed Arms
This household reverently maintains the masterwork weapons of former ages, their power undimmed.

Add 6" to the maximum Range characteristic of ranged weapons a model with this tradition is equipped with that have an unmodified Range characteristic of 24" or more. Add 2" to the maximum Range characteristic of all other ranged weapons a model with this tradition is equipped with.

Glorified History
This household strives to maintain its hard-earned prestige.

When a model with this tradition fires Overwatch or is chosen to shoot or fight with, you can re-roll a single hit roll made for that model.

Shattered Empire Stalkers*
This household is adept at using every ridge, ruin and crater to stay one step ahead of the foes' targeters.

When resolving an attack made with a ranged weapon against a model with this tradition by a model that is more than 24" away, it is treated as having the benefit of cover to its saving throw.

Unremitting*
Never ceasing in their prosecution of fell enemies, this household's Knights each unleash torrents of firepower.

When a model with this tradition fires Overwatch or is chosen to shoot with, you can re-roll a single dice when determining the number of attacks that model makes when attacking with a weapon that has a random number of attacks (e.g. Heavy D6).

Slayers of Beasts
A millennia-old culture of hunting the great beasts of their home world has accustomed the Knights of this household to the movements of such hulking brutes.

When resolving an attack made with a melee weapon (excluding titanic feet) by a model with this tradition against a **Vehicle** or **Monster** unit, add 1 to the hit roll.

Hunters of the Unseen*
With auto-sanctified auspex relays – and keen huntsman's eyes – this household roots out its foes.

When resolving an attack made with a ranged weapon by a model with this tradition, the target does not receive the benefit of cover to its saving throw.

Defiant Fury
Incensed by those who dare harm their ancient Knight suits, this household's Nobles' wrath invigorates them.

Whilst a model with this tradition has lost half or more of its wounds, increase its Attacks characteristic by 1.

When resolving an attack made with a melee weapon by a model with this tradition that has lost half or more of its wounds, add 1 to the hit roll.

Stormstriders

Nothing can halt the ever moving Knights of this household, their path punctuated with wrathful strikes .

Add 1" to the Move characteristic of a model with this tradition and always use the top row of its damage table when determining its Move characteristic, regardless of how many wounds it has left.

Hounds of War

This household's Armiger pilots are nimble combatants, using feints and sudden ripostes to ravage the enemy.

An **ARMIGER CLASS** model with this tradition can either shoot or charge in a turn in which it Fell Back. If it shoots, when resolving an attack made by that model in the Shooting phase of that turn, subtract 1 from the hit roll.

Noble Combatants

Drilled in the honourable art of duelling, every blade thrust and crushing swipe of this household's Knights is a breathtaking study in finesse.

When resolving an attack made with a melee weapon (excluding titanic feet) by a model with this tradition, an unmodified hit roll of 6 scores 1 additional hit.

Exacting Charge

During every thunderous step of their charge, the Nobles of this household are utterly focused. When their strike hits home, it is with piercing precision.

If a model with this tradition makes a charge move, is charged or performs a Heroic Intervention, the Armour Penetration characteristic of melee weapons that model is equipped with (excluding titanic feet) is improved by 1 until the end of the turn (e.g. AP 0 becomes AP -1).

Honoured Sacristans*

The Sacristans of this household are amongst the greatest of their calling, maintaining the iron-hard skin of their masters' Knights with esoteric techniques.

When resolving an attack made with a weapon that has an Armour Penetration characteristic of -1 against a model with this tradition, that weapon is treated as having an Armour Penetration characteristic of 0.

Survivors of Strife*

The home world of this household fared better than some during the Age of Strife, thus its Knight suits remain girded with ancient protective technologies thought lost.

Add 1 to the Wounds characteristic of **ARMIGER CLASS** models with this tradition. Add 2 to the Wounds characteristic of all other models with this tradition.

Pains of Old Night*

Deep were the wounds suffered by this household when they fought the terrors of Old Night, and the fires lit in that time continue to burn within their hearts.

When resolving an attack made by a model with this tradition against a **PSYKER** or **DAEMON** unit, re-roll a wound roll of 1.

Machine Focus*

The Nobles of this household are minutely attuned to the fabric and soul of their Knight suits, in a seamless fusion of man and machine that refines their sensorium.

When resolving an attack made by a model with this tradition that is subject to any negative hit roll modifiers, add 1 to the hit roll.

Guardians of the Frontier

Long have the Knights of this household fought upon the fringes against innumerable odds and the rapacious hunger that lurks beyond civilisation.

Whilst a model with this tradition is within 1" of any enemy units that contain 11 or more models, increase its Attacks characteristic by 1.

Front-line Fighters

The Knights of this household unleash the full power of their fury only when in the very heart of the enemy, honour demanding no less of their Nobles.

When resolving an attack made with a ranged weapon by a model with this tradition against a unit within 12", improve the Armour Penetration characteristic of that weapon by 1 for that attack (e.g. AP 0 becomes AP -1).

Steel-sinewed Aim

Striding full pelt into their enemies, the Knights of this household direct even indiscriminate weapons with a rare calm and preternatural stability.

Models with this tradition do not suffer the penalties to their hit rolls for Advancing and shooting Assault weapons.

Sanctified Armour

Every immense greave, helm and tilting shield carried by the Knights of this household are thrice-blessed against the fell sorceries of witches and daemonkin.

When a model with this tradition would lose a wound in the Psychic phase, roll one D6; on a 5+ that wound is not lost.

QUESTOR ALLEGIANCE OATHS

When the Knight worlds were rediscovered after the isolation and terror of the Age of Strife, there was a race for their allegiance between the Imperial Administratum and the Cult Mechanicus. Fealty and integrity are so intrinsic to the knightly households that these oaths remain a lynchpin of their existence millennia later.

Imperial Knights owe their allegiance to either the Imperium of Man or the Machine Cult of the Adeptus Mechanicus. This is represented by the <QUESTOR ALLEGIANCE> keyword, as described in *Codex: Imperial Knights*. The rules presented over the following pages are new rules for Imperial Knights based on their choice of allegiance.

If your army is Battle-forged, units in an IMPERIAL KNIGHTS Super-heavy Detachment can gain a Questor Allegiance Oath so long as every unit in that Detachment has the same <QUESTOR ALLEGIANCE>. If every unit in that Detachment is QUESTOR MECHANICUS, they can gain the Sacristan Pledge Questor Allegiance Oath. If every unit in that Detachment is QUESTOR IMPERIALIS, they can gain the Vow of Honour Questor Allegiance Oath.

Questor Mechanicus: Sacristan Pledge

Those households that swear allegiance to the Adeptus Mechanicus preserve the mutual pledge that saw their Knight worlds raised out of technological oblivion. Their failing Knight suits were restored and the arcane knowledge granted to the formative Sacristan orders raised them to a holy perfection of function.

At the start of your turn, a model with this Questor Allegiance Oath regains 1 lost wound.

Questor Imperialis: Vow of Honour

These households pledged their undying allegiance to the Emperor, and swore to defend the Imperium with neither question nor hesitation. In the millennia since, their Knights have endured hardships and fought monstrous foes in fulfillment of those ancient oaths.

Add 1 to Advance and charge rolls made for a model with this Questor Allegiance Oath. This is not cumulative with any other modifiers (e.g. Landstrider).

QUESTOR ALLEGIANCE WARLORD TRAITS

If an **Imperial Knights Character** model is your Warlord, you can use a Questor Allegiance Warlord Traits tables to determine what Warlord Trait they have instead of those presented in other publications. You can only use the Warlord Traits table that is relative to the model's <Questor Allegiance>. Either roll one D3 to randomly generate one, or you can select one.

QUESTOR MECHANICUS WARLORD TRAITS

1. PARAGON OF THE OMNISSIAH
This Warlord is a champion of the Machine God, a noble exemplar shielding the forge worlds from harm. The Omnissiah empowers their Knight's core with a burning zeal that cannot be quenched.

Add 2 to this Warlord's Wounds characteristic.

2. COLD ERADICATION
With an icy and calculating menace, this knightly lord establishes the end of the Omnissiah's foes in violent displays of unremitting firepower.

When determining the number of attacks this Warlord makes with a weapon that has a random number of attacks (e.g. Heavy D6), roll one additional dice and discard one of the dice.

3. CALCULATED TARGETING
Judging their foes' honour as swiftly and instinctively as they judge targeting data and fire arc parabola, this Warlord has yet to pardon any.

When resolving an attack made with a ranged weapon by this Warlord (excluding Overwatch), an unmodified hit roll of 4+ is always successful.

QUESTOR IMPERIALIS WARLORD TRAITS

1. REVERED KNIGHT
Never hesitating before honourless invaders, the Warlord is beheld as a towering and monolithic incarnation of the Imperium made manifest.

This Warlord always fights first in the Fight phase, even if it did not charge. If the enemy has units that have charged or that have a similar ability, then alternate choosing units to fight with, starting with the player whose turn is taking place.

2. STRIKE AND SHIELD
Embodying their vow to defend the Emperor's realm, this Warlord parries his enemies with masterful strokes, denying them an easy blow.

When resolving an attack made with a melee weapon against this Warlord, subtract 1 from the hit roll. Whilst an enemy unit is within 1" of this Warlord, subtract 1 from the Attacks characteristic of each **Vehicle** or **Monster** model in that unit.

3. TIRELESS DUTY
Mortal enemies hold little fear for those whose only failure would be to balk, and this Warlord dives into the thick of the fray without hesitation.

This Warlord can perform a Heroic Intervention if there are any enemy units within 6" of it instead of 3", and when doing so can move up to 6" instead of 3".

CHAOS KNIGHTS

'This degenerate peerage know nothing of honour, nothing of loyalty or endurance to the bitterest end. Let their so-called Knights' last sight be true nobility, as we tear them apart. Slowly.'

- *Zair Tedorok,*
'The Tormentor'

DREAD LORDS OF RUINATION

The rules in this section supplement those found in *Codex: Chaos Knights* and can be used in any open play, narrative play or matched play game. They include new rules for dread households, Warlord Traits, Stratagems, Artefacts of Tyranny and Household Bond abilities for dread households of your own creation.

Name Generator

Opposite you will find a name generator. This helpful tool ensures you should have no trouble naming your pilots and their Knights, so your enemies will never forget who delivered their ruination.

Dread Households

In this section you will find expanded rules for your Chaos Knights models, allowing you to declare which of the dread households that Knight belongs to. Some of these will be Iconoclast households, those who have renounced their vows and taken up arms against their former allies. Others are Infernal households, fusing the powers of the warp with the techno-heresy of the Dark Mechanicum. Whatever their greater allegiance, both of these bring unique abilities to the battlefield and the persecution of their enemies.

On pages 68-71 you will find a full set of rules for the five Chaos Knight households featured in *Codex: Chaos Knights*. These include a Household Bond for each of these storied households. Household Bonds is a new ability that allows your household to behave in distinct and unique ways on the battlefield and exemplify that household's particular methods of war. You will also find a new Warlord Trait, Relic and Stratagem for each of these households, helping to capture the predilections and practices of these dread combatants.

If the household you have chosen for your Chaos Knights is not one of the ones featured, you can instead use the rules presented on pages 72-73 to create a Household Bond of your own devising from the abilities listed. This ensures that your particular household is able to act on the battlefield according to the lore.

'I can sense Dam Ferona sometimes. When Ruination is impassioned, when slaughter is all we see and the Throne sings in violent harmony, I can hear her screams: tortured and in terror, by the sound. The Throne finds me a far more suitable match. I have nothing to fear.'

- *Dam Nyatal, current pilot of Ruination*

CHAOS KNIGHTS NAME GENERATOR

The Fallen Nobles who pilot Chaos Knight suits usually belong to a Dread Household, and will share that line's family name. Some Dread Households use the titles sir and lady to honour those who pilot Knight suits, while many have their own traditions, using dom, lord, magnate and countless others. Some use elements such as Ilka, Zu or Riga to denote a Fallen Noble is 'of' a particular Dread Household. If you wish to randomly generate a personal name for your Fallen Nobles and a name for their Knight suit, you can roll a D66 and consult the tables below. To roll a D66, simply roll two D6, one after the other – the first represents tens, and the second represents digits, giving you a result between 11 and 66.

D66	FALLEN NOBLE'S NAME
11	Elsyr
12	Brenn XCI
13	Bahras
14	Kohn 'the Damned'
15	Marta
16	Annalric
21	Brynhild
22	Shan
23	Xitra CDV
24	Reynalt
25	Dinatis
26	Bohemont 'the Butcher'
31	Kyoptis
32	Pons
33	Decima
34	Roi-Mene
35	Lukia
36	Birtaran
41	Khonstanz
42	Trevenek LVI
43	Mohgera
44	Kaligius
45	Malfisende
46	Abesh
51	'Khemys' Sibilla
52	Virnet XI
53	Nyatal
54	Waersk
55	Ferona
56	Gelki
61	Isoltor
62	Kohor
63	El'hena
64	Obidar
65	Nenna 'the Infernal Raptora'
66	Ifanor

D66	KNIGHT SUIT'S NAME
11	Abhorrentis
12	Nulborex
13	Bringer of Extinction
14	Sedevitalis
15	Thunderhead
16	Dex Malvolo
21	Iron Malice
22	Honour Blight
23	Obstinate Will
24	Betrayer's House
25	Unflinching Wrath
26	Fatewarden
31	Eternal Dread
32	Khorifex
33	Mantle of Ash
34	Paean of Hunger
35	Scorched Fury
36	Bilgpore
41	The Burning Sky
42	Bond Infernal
43	Drixia's Maul
44	Toll of Agony
45	Prey Seeker
46	Insanity of Pruskia
51	The Killing Oath
52	Clawed Caress
53	Tenacious Blade
54	Terrorfel
55	Incarnate Slaughter
56	Dementis Ax
61	Empyrean Scythe
62	Despotic Margravate
63	Litany of Destruction
64	Death's Sabre
65	Hope's Shroud
66	Eternal Avarice

DREAD HOUSEHOLDS OF INFAMY

The dread households that have forsaken their vows come from across the length and breadth of the Imperium. Their particular skills and specialisms are as wide ranging as their reasons for reneging on their oaths of fealty, but all are an equally deadly threat to the realm they previously fought to defend.

If your army is Battle-forged, all **Chaos Knights** models in your army (other than **Dreadblades**, as described in *Codex: Chaos Knights*) gain the **<Dread Household>** Faction keyword. When you include such a unit in your army, you must nominate which household that unit is from. You then simply replace the **<Dread Household>** keyword on that unit's datasheet with the name of your chosen household. If the unit has the **Iconoclast Household** keyword, it must come from an Iconoclast household that owes allegiance only to themselves and their own domains; if the unit has the **Infernal Household** keyword, it must come from a household that owes allegiance to the Dark Mechanicum. You can use any of the households that you have read about, or you can make up your own.

If your army is Battle-forged, all units in a **Chaos Knights** Super-heavy Detachment (other than **Dreadblade** units) must be from the same dread household, but all such models will gain a Household Bond. The Bond gained depends upon the household they are drawn from, as shown on the following pages. For example, such **House Lucaris** units gain the Virtue Through Strength bond.

In order to be given any of the Household Bonds listed here, a model must have the appropriate **<Questor Traitoris>** keyword.

- **House Lucaris**, **House Herpetrax** and **House Khymere** can only be selected for models with the **Iconoclast Household** keyword.

- **House Vextrix** and **House Khomentis** may only be selected for models which have the **Infernal Household** keyword.

The following sets of rules apply to each of the houses listed in *Codex: Chaos Knights*. Each contains a Household Bond, Warlord Trait, Artefact of Tyranny and Stratagem that can only be used by models with the appropriate dread household keyword.

If you have chosen a household that does not have an associated Household Bond, you must use the rules described on pages 72-73 to create a Household Bond of your own.

HOUSE HERPETRAX
Household Bond
Dauntless

The Fallen Nobles of House Herpetrax are indomitable, refusing to fall even as their Knight suits burn around them.

Add 2 to the Wounds characteristic of models with this bond (add 1 instead if that model is a **War Dog**).

Warlord Trait

If a **House Herpetrax Character** is your Warlord, you can give them the following Warlord Trait instead of one of the ones listed on page 70 of *Codex: Chaos Knights*.

Bound to None

This warlord has stared down even the most terrifying Daemons of the warp, and is as unwilling to bend the knee before the ineffable as before any other mortal.

The first time this Warlord is destroyed, if it does not explode, roll one D6 at the end of the phase; on a 4+ return this model to play with D3 wounds remaining, placing it as close as possible to its previous position and more than 1" away from any enemy models.

Artefact of Tyranny
Crown of Jedathra

This Throne Mechanicum enhances the natural agility and reactions of the Fallen Noble who bonds with it, allowing them to sidestep the clumsy attacks of their rivals.

House Herpetrax model only. When resolving an attack with a melee weapon against a model with this Relic, subtract 1 from the hit roll.

WARPING AURA
House Herpetrax Stratagem

To stay too long in the presence of the Knights of House Herpetrax is to invite an agonising death.

Use this Stratagem at the end of the Fight phase. Select one **House Herpetrax** model from your army. Roll one D6 for each enemy unit within 1" of that model; on a 4+ that unit suffers 1 mortal wound,

HOUSE LUCARIS
HOUSEHOLD BOND
Virtue Through Strength

The Fallen Nobles of House Lucaris fight only to destroy each enemy before them, to trample their bodies into the dirt and to stride onwards over their annihilated foe.

When resolving an attack made with a melee weapon by a model with this bond in a turn in which that model's unit made a charge move, was charged or performed a Heroic Intervention, add 1 to the hit roll.

WARLORD TRAIT

If a **HOUSE LUCARIS CHARACTER** is your Warlord, you can give them the following Warlord Trait instead of one of the ones listed on page 70 of *Codex: Chaos Knights.*

Strike First, Strike Often

The knightly lords of House Lucaris vie with each other for the honour of being the first to spill the blood of the enemy. In battle, they strike with a lightning speed unexpected of such large war machines.

This Warlord always fights first in the Fight phase, even if it did not charge. If the enemy has units that have charged, or that have a similar ability, then alternate choosing units to fight with, starting with the player whose turn is taking place.

ARTEFACT OF TYRANNY
Serpentstrike

These potent relic weapons of Morda Prime mimic the serpent that is the sigil of House Lucaris, lashing out in tandem to deal the killing blow to any who come within striking distance.

HOUSE LUCARIS model with two twin meltaguns only. This Relic replaces two twin meltaguns and has the following profile:

WEAPON	RANGE	TYPE	S	AP	D
Serpentstrike	12"	Assault 4	9	-4	D6

Abilities: When resolving an attack made with this weapon, roll two D6 when inflicting damage with it and discard one of the results.

1CP

TRAMPLE THEM
House Lucaris Stratagem
House Lucaris is renowned for its charges, thundering into enemy lines with overwhelming force.

Use this Stratagem after a **HOUSE LUCARIS** unit has moved across any enemy units. Select one enemy unit that was moved across and roll one D6; on a 1, nothing happens. On a 2-5, that unit suffers D3 mortal wounds. On a 6, that unit suffers D6 mortal wounds.

Ifanor, Bringer of Extinction
Since bonding with Ifanor, Bringer of Extinction has waged a merciless war against the loyalist Knights of House Krast.

Elsyr, Thunderhead
The impetuous Lady Elsyr and her Knight Despoiler, Thunderhead, are often first of their lance to engage the enemy.

HOUSE KHYMERE
Household Bond
Rampant Cruelty

The Fallen Nobles of House Khymere take great pleasure in visiting destruction on those who cannot defend themselves, the breadth of their betrayal magnified by their exile in the warp.

When resolving an attack made with a melee weapon (excluding titanic feet) by a model with this bond, re-roll a wound roll of 1.

Warlord Trait

If a **House Khymere Character** is your Warlord, you can give them the following Warlord Trait instead of one of the ones listed on page 70 of *Codex: Chaos Knights*.

Maddened Cries

The warlord's hideously twisted Knight suit broadcasts their deranged rantings as they crash into the enemy line, sending their foes fleeing in terror.

When a Morale test is taken for an enemy unit within 12" of this Warlord, roll one additional D6 and discard the lowest dice result. If both dice results are the same, select one of them to discard.

Artefact of Tyranny
Annihilatum

This corrupted conflagration cannon exhales warp-infused fire from its grotesque barrels. This torrent of unreality drags the seared souls of its victims straight into the warp.

House Khymere model with a conflagration cannon only. This Relic replaces a conflagration cannon and has the following profile:

WEAPON	RANGE	TYPE	S	AP	D
Annihilatum	18"	Assault 3D6	7	-2	3

Abilities: When resolving an attack made with this weapon, do not make a hit roll: it automatically scores a hit.

2CP
FURY OF SURTR'S WAKE
House Khymere Stratagem

The Fallen Nobles of House Khymere have adapted their towering steeds to store excess heat in specialised combustion chambers before unleashing it from every vent as a roiling wave of flame, incinerating all who are caught in the blast.

Use this Stratagem in your Shooting phase. Select one **House Khymere** model from your army. Roll one D6 for each enemy unit within 3" of that model; on a 4+, that enemy unit suffers D3 mortal wounds.

HOUSE VEXTRIX
Household Bond
Titankin

Trained and adapted to perform to the high standards set by their Legio Mortis allies, the Knights of House Vextrix persecute the enemy with incredible tenacity.

When a unit with this bond is chosen to shoot or fight with or fires Overwatch, you can re-roll a single hit roll and a single wound roll made for that unit.

Warlord Trait

If a **House Vextrix Character** is your Warlord, you can give them the following Warlord Trait instead of one of the ones listed on page 70 of *Codex: Chaos Knights*.

Favour of the Dark Mechanicum

This warlord has been bionically augmented with a series of mecha-tendrils that permeate the mechanisms of their Knight suit. If damaged, they can effect simple repairs without breaking their focus.

At the start of your Movement phase, this Warlord regains 1 lost wound.

Artefact of Tyranny
Heretek Power Core

Merging daemonically infused power coils with forbidden xenos bio-phase shards, the Heretek Power Core pushes the Knight's destructive potential to even greater heights.

House Vextrix model only. Add 1" to the Move characteristic of a model with this Relic. In addition, add 1 to the Damage characteristic of the reaper chainsword or thunderstrike gauntlet of a model with this Relic. When a model with this Relic is destroyed, add 1 to any dice rolled to see if that model explodes.

2CP
INTERCEPTION ARRAY
House Vextrix Stratagem

Reaching out with their mind and activating a xeno-tech interception array built into their Knight's sensorium, the Fallen Noble is bombarded with a flurry of information that allows them to predict the movements of even the most elusive foe.

Use this Stratagem at the start of your Shooting phase. Select one **House Vextrix** model from your army. Until the end of the phase, when resolving an attack made with a ranged weapon by this model, ignore hit roll modifiers and Ballistic Skill modifiers.

HOUSE KHOMENTIS
HOUSEHOLD BOND
Profane Symbiosis

Having bartered away their souls to Daemons infesting their Throne Mechanicum, the Fallen Nobles of House Khomentis will often let the feral instincts of these immaterial creatures come to the fore.

Whilst a model with this bond has lost half or more of its wounds, add 1 to its Attacks characteristic and when resolving an attack made with a melee weapon by that model, add 1 to the hit roll. In addition, when a model with this bond would lose a wound in the Psychic phase, roll one D6; on a 5+ that wound is not lost.

WARLORD TRAIT

If a **HOUSE KHOMENTIS CHARACTER** is your Warlord, you can give them the following Warlord Trait instead of one of the ones listed on page 70 of *Codex: Chaos Knights*.

Dread Hunter

This dark lord tracks his foes with the patient eye of one who has hunted the most resilient and abhorrent Daemonic prey, lining up the perfect aim before unleashing the killing shot.

Once per game, at the start of the Shooting phase, you can declare this Warlord will make a killing strike. If you do, select one ranged weapon this Warlord is equipped with. Until the end of the turn, add 1 to the Damage characteristic of that weapon, and when resolving an attack made with that weapon, you can re-roll hit rolls and wound rolls.

ARTEFACT OF TYRANNY
Daemonic Shrike

When released from the Fallen Noble's Throne Mechanicum, this predatory spirit will streak towards the foe and learn its every weakness, before being dragged back into bondage and forced to reveal its newfound knowledge to its dread master.

HOUSE KHOMENTIS model only. At the start of the Shooting phase, select one enemy unit within 18" of a model with this Relic. Until the end of the turn, when resolving an attack made by a model with this Relic, improve the Armour Penetration characteristic of that weapon by 1 for that attack.

1CP
ENCIRCLING HOUNDS
House Khomentis Stratagem

Following ancient hunting tradition, the Fallen Nobles of House Khomentis send their faster vassals to circle behind the enemy and drive them onto their masters' guns and blades.

Use this Stratagem during deployment. Select one **HOUSE KHOMENTIS WAR DOGS** unit from your army. You can set up this unit encircling the foe, instead of setting it up on the battlefield. If you do, at the end of one of your Movement phases you can set up this unit anywhere on the battlefield that is within 6" of a battlefield edge and more than 9" from any enemy models. The War Dogs Vehicle Squadron ability only takes effect when this unit is set up on the battlefield, not when it is set up encircling the foe. You can only use this Stratagem once per battle.

Dinatis, Tenacious Blade
The frenetic daemonic entities infesting Dinatis cause Tenacious Blade's reaper chainsword to whir ceaselessly.

Abesh, the Killing Oath
Masters of the persistent hunt, Abesh and the Killing Oath will wade through entire war zones in pursuit of their marked target.

DREAD HOUSEHOLD BONDS

The Dread Households presented on the previous pages are not the only ones to have reneged on their oaths of allegiance to the Imperium. Chaos Knights from across the galaxy have renounced their vows and taken up arms against their former allies in the name of domination, spoils, vengeance or in the pursuit of long-lost honour.

The previous section states how Chaos Knights units can gain the <DREAD HOUSEHOLD> keyword, and can then substitute that for the name of the household that Knight is taken from. If your chosen household does not have an associated Household Bond listed in the previous section, you can instead create its Household Bond by selecting two of the abilities from the list presented here that best represent the background and fighting traditions of your household.

The usual rules for Household Bonds apply with the following additions:

- All units in a CHAOS KNIGHTS Super-heavy Detachment (other than DREADBLADE units) must have the same <QUESTOR TRAITORIS> keyword.
- Any rules marked with an asterisk (*) count as two selections.

Endless Torment*
This dread household's scions are renowned and feared for laying down an unremitting barrage of fire.

When a model with this bond fires Overwatch or is chosen to shoot with, you can re-roll a single dice when determining the number of attacks that model makes when attacking with a weapon that has a random number of attacks (e.g. Heavy D6).

Pinpoint Cruelty
The Fallen Nobles of this dread household are masters of finding the enemy's weak points and cause the most pain.

When a model with this bond fires Overwatch or is chosen to shoot or fight with, you can re-roll a single dice when determining damage as a result of those attacks.

Infamous Heredity
Ostensibly, this dread household proudly preserves and emulates the richly gilded deeds of notorious past warriors of their line. In truth each Fallen Noble seeks to outdo them and replace their name with their own.

When a model with this bond fires Overwatch or is chosen to shoot or fight with, you can re-roll a single hit roll made for that model.

Gheists of Ruin*
The Knights of this dread household utilise cover to stalk their terrified prey like titanic gheists among broken ruins.

When resolving an attack made with a ranged weapon against a model with this bond by a model that is more than 24" away, it is treated as having the benefit of cover to its saving throw.

Slayers of Kings
These Knights stand toe to toe with the largest foes; the greater the kill, the more satisfying.

When resolving an attack made with a melee weapon (excluding titanic feet) by a model with this bond against a VEHICLE or MONSTER unit, add 1 to the hit roll.

Dark Forging
Pacts with the most powerful soul forges ensure a supply of weapons of the highest quality to this dread household.

Add 6" to the maximum Range characteristic of ranged weapons a model with this bond is equipped with that have an unmodified Range characteristic of 24" or more. Add 2" to the maximum Range characteristic of all other ranged weapons a model with this bond is equipped with.

Warp Vision*
Infernally powered optics allow these Knights to detect and target their foes' animating essence, even when their bodies are hidden.

When resolving an attack made with a ranged weapon by a model with this bond, the target does not receive the benefit to its saving throw as a result of cover.

Pride-fuelled Fury
Any foe with the defiance and power to harm them only leads these Knights to even greater acts of violence.

Whilst a model with this bond has lost half or more of its wounds, increase its Attacks characteristic by 1. When resolving an attack made with a melee weapon by a model with this bond that has lost half or more of its wounds, add 1 to the hit roll.

Abominable Constitution

Hellforged power cores propel these Knights at an incredible pace, even as their damaged actuators and gyro-stabilised drivers are reforged by corrupted energies.

Increase the Move characteristic of a model with this bond by 1" and always use the top row of its damage table when determining its Move characteristic, regardless of how many wounds it has left.

Harrying Packs

This dread household compels their War Dog pilots to shrink back and then strike time and again, drawing the enemy to their masters.

A **War Dog** model with this bond can either shoot or charge in a turn in which it Fell Back. If it shoots, when resolving an attack made by that model in the Shooting phase of that turn, subtract 1 from the hit roll.

Frenzied Attackers

These Knights sweep into the heart of the enemy lines, beweaponed limbs flailing in a whirlwind of gore.

When resolving an attack made with a melee weapon (excluding Titanic Feet) by a model with this bond, an unmodified hit roll of 6 scores 1 additional hit.

Hate-driven Charge

The Knights of this dread household wade into the foe, enmity and malice powering crushing blows against anything within reach.

If a model with this bond makes a charge move, is charged or performs a Heroic Intervention, the Armour Penetration characteristic of melee weapons that model is equipped with (excluding Titanic Feet) is improved by 1 until the end of the turn (e.g. AP 0 becomes AP -1).

Enlightened Idolators*

This dread household maintains a cabal of Idolators who are renowned for their craft and forbidden knowledge, using dread esoterica to shield the Knights from harm.

When resolving an attack made with a weapon that has an Armour Penetration characteristic of -1 against a model with this bond, that weapon is treated as having an Armour Penetration characteristic of 0.

Hellforged Construction*

Reinforced with warp-infused materials and sacrificial offerings, these Knights can withstand savage punishment.

Add 1 to the Wounds characteristic of **War Dog** models with this bond. Add 2 to the Wounds characteristic of all other models with this bond.

Vengeful Outcasts*

Whether this dread household was betrayed or neglected by the Imperium, suffered slavery at Terra's hand or were compelled to abandon their honour, they have never forgotten, nor forgiven.

When resolving an attack made by a model with this bond against an **Imperium** unit, you can re-roll a wound roll of 1.

Heretical System-bond*

The pilots of this dread household are a terrifying fusion of flesh and machine, unable to leave their Knight suit till death – or something darker – takes them. Yet such a bond offers instinctive reflexes and singular precision.

When resolving an attack made by a model with this bond that is subject to any negative hit roll modifiers, add 1 to the hit roll.

Loathing for the Masses

These Knights delight in sweeping their barbed and bladed limbs through swathes of the enemy, sending broken bodies tumbling through the air, for they are nothing but a virulent stain compared to the majesty of a Knight.

Whilst a model with this bond is within 1" of any enemy units that contain 11 or more models, increase its Attacks characteristic by 1.

Bold Tyrants

The Knights of this dread household stride into the very teeth of the enemy, guns blazing, where they can witness first-hand the terrible results of their full power.

When resolving an attack made with a ranged weapon by a model with this bond against a unit within 12", improve the Armour Penetration characteristic of that weapon by 1 for that attack (e.g. AP 0 becomes AP -1).

Rapid Offense

These swift attackers are adept at firing on the move, partitioning off a sliver of consciousness to select and destroy targets of opportunity.

Models with this bond do not suffer the penalties to their hit rolls for Advancing and shooting Assault weapons.

Unhallowed Inscriptions

The hulls of these Knights are covered with indecipherable runic scrawl, invoking dark powers to keep enemy magics at bay.

When a model with this bond would lose a wound in the Psychic phase, roll one D6; on a 5+ that wound is not lost.

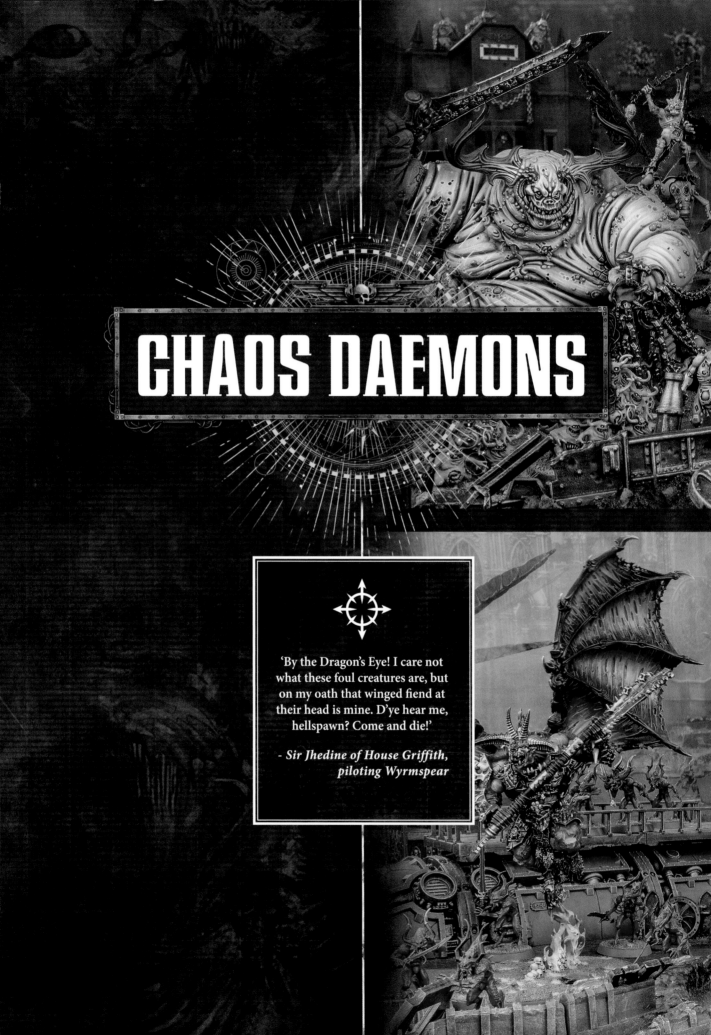

CHAOS DAEMONS

'By the Dragon's Eye! I care not what these foul creatures are, but on my oath that winged fiend at their head is mine. D'ye hear me, hellspawn? Come and die!'

- Sir Jhedine of House Griffith, piloting Wyrmspear

LORDS OF THE WARP

The rules in this section supplement those found in *Codex: Chaos Daemons* and can be used in any open play, narrative play or matched play battle. You'll find new and updated datasheets for Chaos Daemons models, new Stratagems that can be used by Chaos Daemons players, and collection of new rules that allow you to represent Exalted Greater Daemons – amongst the most deadly and feared of the Dark Gods' immortal champions.

Datasheets

Pages 77-89 present new and updated units available to the Chaos Daemons. You will find a detailed account of their background and fighting style, followed by datasheets to use these new units in your games of Warhammer 40,000. If a datasheet appears in both this book and in a previous publications (e.g. *Codex: Chaos Daemons*) the datasheets found in this publication supersede any that already exist. The points values for these units are presented in the table below for use in matched play or games that use a points limit.

Stratagems

If your army is Battle-forged and includes any Chaos Daemons Detachments – that is, any Detachment that only includes units with both the **Chaos** and **Daemon** Faction keywords – the Stratagems on page 92-93 can be used in addition to those presented in *Codex: Chaos Daemons*.

Exalted Greater Daemons

This section (pg 94-101) introduces upgrades to many Greater Daemons models. For each of the Greater Daemons detailed in this section, you will find:

- A Stratagem that upgrades a Greater Daemon to be Exalted and gifts them with new abilities. If you have an army roster, specify on it which model(s) you have used these Stratagems on.

- A number of powerful Hellforged Artefacts that can only be wielded by **Exalted** Greater Daemons. Some are weapons that replace one of the model's existing weapons. Where this is the case, if you are playing a matched play battle, or otherwise using points values, you must still pay the cost of the weapon that is being replaced. Write down any Hellforged Artefacts your models have on your army roster.

Name Generator

On pages 102-103 you will find useful tools to help you establish the names of your Daemons, further building the fearsome reputation of the denizens of the warp.

UNIT	MODELS PER UNIT	POINTS PER MODEL (Including weapons)
Bloodcrushers	3-12	40
Contorted Epitome	1	195
Fiends	1-9	37
Flesh Hounds	5-20	15 (Gore Hound is 24)
Herald of Slaanesh on Exalted Seeker Chariot	1	120
Herald of Slaanesh on Hellflayer	1	100
Herald of Slaanesh on Seeker Chariot	1	90
Horrors	10-30	
- Blue Horrors		5
- Pair of Brimstone Horrors		3
- Pink Horrors		7
- Iridescent Horror		7
Infernal Enrapturess	1	70
Keeper of Secrets with:		
- Living whip	1	210
- Ritual knife	1	210
- Shining aegis	1	220
- Sinistrous hand	1	210
Seekers	5-20	15
Shalaxi Helbane with:		
- Living whip	1	220
- Shining aegis	1	230
Syll'Esske, the Vengeful Allegiance	1	210
OTHER WARGEAR	**POINTS PER ITEM**	
Daemonic Icon	15	
Instrument of Chaos	10	

Matched Play Rule – Daemonic Jealousy: In a matched play game, you can only select each Exalted ability once. This does not prevent other **Exalted** Greater Daemons from having the same Exalted ability (or abilities), but only if they have been rolled for randomly. If you are randomly rolling for Exalted abilities, write 'Random' on your army list for that unit and roll the dice before the battle in front of your opponent.

KEEPERS OF SECRETS

The six-limbed abominations that are Slaanesh's Greater Daemons are as loathsome as they are beguiling. Keepers of Secrets are sickeningly fast, inventively violent and possessed of a dark intelligence. With silvered lies and a seductive aura, victims recognise too late their snapping claws and razor-edged blades.

When a Keeper of Secrets bursts from the warp, it is in a riot of sensation. Clashing sounds and sickening colours are accentuated by cloying scents. Through this discord, the Daemon's arcane powers manifest as pleasure and pain. Waves of suffering and psychic terror accompany its blade strikes, creating an orgy of slaughter.

Few mortals survive long in the presence of a Keeper of Secrets, and fewer still retain any shred of sanity. It embodies the opposed allure and repulsiveness of Slaanesh. Even veterans inured to battlefield horror are struck dumb by its awe-inspiring beauty as they quail in terror at the Daemon's repulsive perversity. Its lithe and pale limbs

seem sculpted from the finest unblemished marble, ending in cruelly barbed talons and bestial hooves. Delicate jewels are worn that reflect dazzling hues, yet contain convulsing souls in abject torment. Its eyes hold the promise of every desire, pools of mesmeric degradation in which the unwary easily drown.

Keepers of Secrets are Slaanesh's force of ultimate violence, and are as varied as the Dark Prince's shifting whims. The Greater Daemons aim to savour and perfect every experience and when drawn to battlefields of slaughter, they indulge in a myriad expressions of torment. Long blades are woven in quicksilver arcs, cords of sentient sinew lash like

lightning and stabbing claws coax out arterial sprays of blood.

Each of these graceful movements belie a hideous strength that tears through armourplas and crushes skulls. Every lightning-fast blow is placed with precision, every cut measured to inflict pain in an exquisitely new and vicious manner.

Slaanesh's Greater Daemons feed on emotions; the richer and more extreme the sensation, the greater the satisfaction. Mere proximity to a Keeper of Secrets engenders shameful lust and violent desire. Obsessions and pride overtake stalwart rigour and there are few things more gratifying to them than to corrupt a noble heart.

LEGIONES DAEMONICA

From within the twisting and hellish environs of the warp, legions of daemonic beings surge into realspace to mercilessly slaughter, subjugate and enslave the galaxy at the behest of the Dark Gods of Chaos.

Created from the very stuff of Chaos itself, boundless and infinite, Daemons nonetheless conform to the temperaments, passions and obsessions of the Dark God to whom they owe their existence.

Flesh Hounds of Khorne, for instance, howl with an insatiable bloodlust and relentlessly hunt down the souls of cowards and traitors, while Bloodcrushers are brazen knights, reflecting their creator's aggression and mindless violence. Horrors replicate the mutative and endless forms of their master, Tzeentch, and are magic made manifest, cackling insanely as they hurl gouts of psychic fire. Similarly, Slaanesh's corrupting Heralds, hunting Seekers and nightmarish Fiends each extol an aspect of the Dark Prince's desires.

SHALAXI HELBANE

One of the favoured thralls of Slaanesh, Shalaxi Helbane epitomises an obsession with the hunt. The towering Keeper of Secrets tracks and pursues the greatest prey from one side of the galaxy to the other, never stopping or allowing their quarry a moment's respite before the blissful conclusion of the chase. Those who believe they can elude the hunter are driven to obsession.

Some desperately flee for their whole lives, their existence given over to the overwhelming need to escape. Others are driven to amass the power and armies with which to confront the inexorable approach. The most loathsome are those compelled into the worship of Slaanesh itself in a quest to survive.

Those whose actions most counter Slaanesh's works become the objects of Helbane's unstoppable pursuit and are often the greatest of their kind. Imperial Knights, Tyranid monstrosities and the champions of rival Chaos Gods have all been transfixed upon the Keeper of Secrets' Daemon-forged spear, and Shalaxi holds a special passion for destroying Bloodthirsters, the Greater Daemons of Khorne.

Every aspect of Helbane's fighting style is perfected to counter the largest and most dangerous adversaries, and none ever escape the hunter's keen senses. Shalaxi can see their soul-spoor over vast distances and taste the tang of their cowardice. Victims can feel its gaze as the Daemon nears, their fear only marking them out more sharply.

INFERNAL ENRAPTURESSES

The cacophonic barrage unleashed by an Infernal Enrapturess sets nerves alight, bursts eardrums, ruptures organs and cripples battle tanks. These privileged Daemons make music that resonates across the boundaries of time and space. Their haunting chords lure unwary virtuosos into obsession, culminating in the mortals' transformation into an instrument of diabolical harmonies. The heartstring lyre is strung with the fallen's soul, which endures an eternity of torment at the hands of the Infernal Enrapturess.

These Daemons weave sublime siren songs and excessive atonal fusillades. Their melodies seep through both realspace and the warp, weakening its boundaries and heralding the Legions of Excess. Upon battlefields across the galaxy, Infernal Enrapturesses skilfully draw elated refrains from their horrific instruments in varying frequencies. Enemies are compelled to dance to the jarring cacophonies and differing rhythms, tearing their bodies apart, while long euphonic dirges distil emotion into heart-stopping agony.

SYLL'ESSKE, THE VENGEFUL ALLEGIANCE

The symbiotic pairing at the heart of Syll'Esske's permanent bond is unusual amongst the notoriously fickle servants of Slaanesh, yet was nonetheless born out of an overflow of dark emotion. Syll is a Herald of the Dark Prince obsessed with the gladiatorial mortal devotees who fight for Slaanesh's favour. Esske is one such depraved fighter, raised to daemonhood under Syll's wise patronage. Humiliated and spurned by the Daemons of Slaanesh's court, the two joined forces, unleashed their rage and murderous frenzy upon the other Daemons. Swearing a damning pact, they bound themselves inextricably for eternity.

They are compelled to fight as one, an addiction neither is willing or able to relinquish, yet this codependency has borne terrible fruit. As Syll'Esske, their combined power and depravity have debased and enslaved countless worlds. Syll's scourging whip flays flesh and armour in spiralling circuits of exultant pain. Esske's curved and double-bladed axe severs the soul in nerve-shredding bliss as easily as it cleaves through solid plascrete. Together, their regal authority and obsessive devotion sees them feared and adored by Daemon and mortal alike.

CONTORTED EPITOMES

Rumours litter the galaxy as to the origin of the fell devices known as Contorted Epitomes, each tale a lie as deadly to the unwary as these constructs and their guardians are. The cultists on Gibril Deltis believe that the greatest artificer of Old Earth fashioned the first, and that the Dark Prince's daemonic servants stole him away to recreate them over and over again for eternity. Whispers on Vakkar, meanwhile, tell of xenos who created them as truth-tellers, but that they saw too much and Slaanesh claimed them.

The living frame and its coiling tendrils are empowered by a warp-spawned sentience, while to each side a favoured Herald attends the device, lashing out with their claws at any who get too close. Between them sits a Mirror of Absorption, greedily devouring psychic energies that would slay its fellow Daemons. Its surface is said to reflect an onlooker's strongest emotions and basest desires. Those whose gaze is caught by the mirror are trapped in an eternal spellbound state – until the living frame's writhing coils and the attendants' barbed claws reach them, that is.

SYLL'ESSKE
THE VENGEFUL ALLEGIANCE

NAME	M	WS	BS	S	T	W	A	Ld	Sv
Syll'Esske	9"	2+	2+	4	6	8	8	9	4+

Syll'Esske is a single model equipped with: scourging whip; Axe of Dominion. You can only include one of this model in your army.

WEAPON	RANGE	TYPE	S	AP	D	ABILITIES
Scourging whip (shooting)	6"	Assault D6	User	-2	1	This weapon can be fired even if there are enemy units within 1" of the bearer, and attacks made with this weapon can target enemy units within 1" of friendly units.
Axe of Dominion	Melee	Melee	+3	-3	3	-
Scourging whip (melee)	Melee	Melee	User	-1	1	Make D3 hit rolls for each attack made with this weapon, instead of 1.

ABILITIES	Daemonic, Quicksilver Swiftness, Daemonic Ritual (see *Codex: Chaos Daemons*)	**Deadly Symbiosis:** When this model is chosen to fight with for the first time in the Fight phase, it can only make attacks with one of its equipped weapons. The first time this model finishes its Consolidation step of the Fight phase, it can immediately fight again, but when it does so all of its attacks must be made with the other weapon (if this model charged this turn, these attacks can still only target units that it declared a charge against in the previous phase).
	Prince of Slaanesh: Re-roll hit rolls of 1 for attacks made by models in friendly **SLAANESH DAEMON** units whilst their unit is within 6" of this model.	
	Locus of Slaanesh: Add 1 to the Strength characteristic of models in **SLAANESH DAEMON** units whilst their unit is within 6" of any friendly models with this ability.	
	Regal Authority: You can re-roll Morale tests taken for friendly **SLAANESH DAEMON** units whilst they are within 6" of this model.	
PSYKER	This model can attempt to manifest one psychic power in your Psychic phase, and attempt to deny one psychic power in your opponent's Psychic phase. It knows *Smite* and two psychic powers from the Slaanesh discipline (see *Codex: Chaos Daemons*).	
FACTION KEYWORDS	**CHAOS, SLAANESH, DAEMON**	
KEYWORDS	**CHARACTER, MONSTER, PSYKER, DAEMONETTE, HERALD OF SLAANESH, DAEMON PRINCE, SYLL'ESSKE**	

SHALAXI HELBANE

DAMAGE

Some of this model's characteristics change as it suffers damage, as shown below:

REMAINING W	M	A	SNAPPING CLAWS
9-16+	14"	6	4
5-8	11"	5	3
1-4	7"	4	2

NAME	M	WS	BS	S	T	W	A	Ld	Sv
Shalaxi Helbane	*	2+	2+	6	7	16	*	10	6+

Shalaxi Helbane is a single model equipped with: living whip; snapping claws; Soulpiercer. You can only include one of this model in your army.

WEAPON	RANGE	TYPE	S	AP	D	ABILITIES
Living whip	6"	Assault 6	6	-2	2	This weapon can be fired even if there are enemy units within 1" of the bearer, and attacks made with this weapon can target enemy units within 1" of friendly units.
Snapping claws	Melee	Melee	User	-3	3	When the bearer fights, it makes a number of additional attacks with this weapon equal to the number shown in its damage table. When resolving an attack made with this weapon, on a wound roll of 6+ this weapon has an Armour Penetration characteristic of -4 for that attack.
Soulpiercer	Melee	Melee	x2	-4	D6	When resolving an attack made with this weapon against a **CHARACTER** unit, on a wound roll of 6+ this weapon has a Damage characteristic of 6 for that attack.

WARGEAR OPTIONS	
	• This model can have a shining aegis instead of being equipped with 1 living whip.

ABILITIES	
	Daemonic, Quicksilver Swiftness, Daemonic Ritual (see *Codex: Chaos Daemons*) **Greater Daemon:** When a Morale test is taken for a friendly **SLAANESH DAEMON** unit within 6" of this model, you can use this model's Leadership characteristic instead of that unit's. **Mesmerising Aura:** When resolving an attack made with a melee weapon against this model, subtract 1 from the hit roll. **Cloak of Constriction:** When resolving an attack made with a melee weapon against this model, subtract 1 from the wound roll. **Delicate Precision:** When resolving an attack made by this model, re-roll a wound roll of 1.	**Shining Aegis:** If this model has a shining aegis, then when it would lose a wound, roll one D6; on a 6 that wound is not lost. If that wound would be lost as a result of a mortal wound, that wound is not lost on a 5+ instead of 6. **Monarch of the Hunt:** This model can perform a Heroic Intervention if there are any enemy units within 6" of it instead of 3" if any of those enemy units is a **CHARACTER**, and when doing so can move up to 6" instead of 3" so long as it ends that move closer to the closest enemy **CHARACTER** model. In addition, when this model makes a pile-in move within 6" of any enemy **CHARACTER** units, it can move up to 6" instead of 3" so long as it ends that move closer to the closest enemy **CHARACTER** model.

PSYKER	This model can attempt to manifest two psychic powers in your Psychic phase and attempt to deny one psychic power in your opponent's Psychic phase. It knows *Smite* and two psychic powers from the Slaanesh discipline (see *Codex: Chaos Daemons*).
FACTION KEYWORDS	**CHAOS, SLAANESH, DAEMON**
KEYWORDS	**CHARACTER, MONSTER, PSYKER, KEEPER OF SECRETS, SHALAXI HELBANE**

INFERNAL ENRAPTURESS

4 POWER

NAME	M	WS	BS	S	T	W	A	Ld	Sv
Infernal Enrapturess	7"	2+	2+	4	3	4	2	8	6+

An Infernal Enrapturess is a single model equipped with: heartstring lyre; ravaging claws.

WEAPON	RANGE	TYPE	S	AP	D	ABILITIES
Heartstring lyre		When you choose this weapon to shoot with, select one of the profiles below.				
- Cacophonous melody	18"	Assault 6	4	-1	1	-
- Euphonic blast	24"	Assault 1	8	-3	3	-
Ravaging claws	Melee	Melee	User	-1	2	When resolving an attack made with this weapon, on a wound roll of 6+ this weapon has an Armour Penetration characteristic of -4 for that attack.

ABILITIES	**Daemonic, Quicksilver Swiftness, Daemonic Ritual** (see *Codex: Chaos Daemons*)
	Discordant Disruption: When a Psychic test is taken for a model within 24" of any enemy models with this ability, that model suffers Perils of the Warp on a roll that includes any doubles.
	Harmonic Alignment: When this model attempts to summon a **Slaanesh Daemon** unit using the Daemonic Ritual ability, add 3 to the summoning roll. In addition, at the start of your turn, roll one D6 for each **Slaanesh** unit from your army that has the **Daemon** Faction keyword and is within 6" of any friendly models with this ability; on a 6 you can return one destroyed model from that unit to the battlefield with all of its wounds remaining, placing it in unit coherency (if the model cannot be placed in this way, it is not returned to the battlefield).

FACTION KEYWORDS	**Chaos, Slaanesh, Daemon**
KEYWORDS	**Character, Infantry, Daemonette, Herald of Slaanesh, Infernal Enrapturess**

CONTORTED EPITOME

10 POWER

NAME	M	WS	BS	S	T	W	A	Ld	Sv
Contorted Epitome	12"	2+	2+	4	5	8	8	8	6+

A Contorted Epitome is a single model equipped with: coiled tentacles; ravaging claws.

WEAPON	RANGE	TYPE	S	AP	D	ABILITIES
Coiled tentacles	Melee	Melee	+1	-2	3	When the bearer fights, it makes 2 additional attacks with this weapon and no more than 2 attacks can be made with this weapon.
Ravaging claws	Melee	Melee	User	-1	2	When resolving an attack made with this weapon, on a wound roll of 6+ this weapon has an Armour Penetration characteristic of -4 for that attack.

ABILITIES	**Daemonic, Quicksilver Swiftness, Daemonic Ritual** (see *Codex: Chaos Daemons*)	**Swallow Energy:** When this model would lose a wound as a result of a mortal wound, roll one D6; on a 2+ that wound is not lost.
	Locus of Slaanesh: Add 1 to the Strength characteristic of models in **Slaanesh Daemon** units whilst their unit is within 6" of any friendly models with this ability.	
		Horrible Fascination: When a unit within 6" of any enemy models with this ability is chosen to Fall Back, roll 3D6; if the total is greater than or equal to that unit's Leadership characteristic, that unit cannot Fall Back this turn.
	Gift of Power: When a Psychic test or Deny the Witch test is taken for this model, add 1 to the total.	

PSYKER	This model can attempt to manifest two psychic powers in your Psychic phase, and attempt to deny two psychic powers in your opponent's Psychic phase. It knows *Smite* and two psychic powers from the Slaanesh discipline (see *Codex: Chaos Daemons*).

FACTION KEYWORDS	**Chaos, Slaanesh, Daemon**
KEYWORDS	**Character, Cavalry, Psyker, Daemonette, Herald of Slaanesh, Contorted Epitome**

KEEPER OF SECRETS

NAME	M	WS	BS	S	T	W	A	Ld	Sv
Keeper of Secrets	*	2+	2+	6	7	16	*	10	6+

DAMAGE

Some of this model's characteristics change as it suffers damage, as shown below:

REMAINING W	M	A	SNAPPING CLAWS
9-16+	12"	6	4
5-8	9"	5	3
1-4	6"	4	2

A Keeper of Secrets is a single model equipped with: snapping claws; witstealer sword. It has a ritual knife.

WEAPON	RANGE	TYPE	S	AP	D	ABILITIES
Living whip	6"	Assault 6	6	-2	2	This weapon can be fired even if there are enemy units within 1" of the bearer, and attacks made with this weapon can target enemy units within 1" of friendly units.
Snapping claws	Melee	Melee	User	-3	3	When the bearer fights, it makes a number of additional attacks with this weapon equal to the number shown in its damage table. When resolving an attack made with this weapon, on a wound roll of 6+ this weapon has an Armour Penetration characteristic of -4 for that attack.
Witstealer sword	Melee	Melee	+2	-3	3	When resolving an attack made by a model that has lost one or more wounds from an attack made with this weapon, subtract 1 from the hit roll.

WARGEAR OPTIONS	• This model can be equipped with 1 living whip instead of having a ritual knife. • This model can have one of the following instead of having a ritual knife: shining aegis; sinistrous hand.

ABILITIES	**Daemonic**, **Quicksilver Swiftness**, **Daemonic Ritual** (see *Codex: Chaos Daemons*) **Greater Daemon:** When a Morale test is taken for a friendly **SLAANESH DAEMON** unit within 6" of this model, you can use this model's Leadership characteristic instead of that unit's. **Delicate Precision:** When resolving an attack made by this model, re-roll a wound roll of 1. **Shining Aegis:** If this model has a shining aegis, then when it would lose a wound, roll one D6; on a 6+ that wound is not lost. If that wound would be lost as a result of a mortal wound, that wound is not lost on a 5+ instead of 6+.	**Ritual Knife:** If this model has a ritual knife, after making a consolidate move, select one enemy unit within 1" of this model and roll one D6; on a 2-5 that unit suffers 1 mortal wound, on a 6 that unit suffers D3 mortal wounds. **Mesmerising Aura:** When resolving an attack made with a melee weapon against this model, subtract 1 from the hit roll. **Sinistrous Hand:** If this model has a sinistrous hand, then at the end of the Fight phase, if any enemy models that are not **VEHICLES** were destroyed as a result of an attack made with a melee weapon by this model that phase, this model regains up to D3 lost wounds.

PSYKER	This model can attempt to manifest two psychic powers in your Psychic phase, and attempt to deny one psychic power in your opponent's Psychic phase. It knows Smite and two psychic powers from the Slaanesh discipline (see *Codex: Chaos Daemons*).

FACTION KEYWORDS	**CHAOS, SLAANESH, DAEMON**
KEYWORDS	**CHARACTER, MONSTER, PSYKER, KEEPER OF SECRETS**

HERALD OF SLAANESH
ON EXALTED SEEKER CHARIOT

DAMAGE
Some of this model's characteristics change as it suffers damage, as shown below:

REMAINING W	M	WS	A
7-12+	12"	2+	8
4-6	10"	3+	6
1-3	8"	4+	4

NAME	M	WS	BS	S	T	W	A	Ld	Sv
Herald of Slaanesh on Exalted Seeker Chariot	*	*	2+	4	5	12	*	8	4+

A Herald of Slaanesh on Exalted Seeker Chariot is a single model equipped with: lashes of torment; ravaging claws; lashing tongues.

WEAPON	RANGE	TYPE	S	AP	D	ABILITIES
Lashes of torment	6"	Assault D6	4	0	1	This weapon can be fired even if there are enemy units within 1" of the bearer, and attacks made with this weapon can target enemy units within 1" of friendly units.
Lashing tongues	Melee	Melee	4	0	1	When the bearer fights, it makes 8 additional attacks with this weapon and no more than 8 attacks can be made with this weapon.
Ravaging claws	Melee	Melee	User	-1	2	When resolving an attack made with this weapon, on a wound roll of 6+ this weapon has an Armour Penetration characteristic of -4 for that attack.

ABILITIES	**Daemonic, Quicksilver Swiftness, Daemonic Ritual** (see *Codex: Chaos Daemons*)
	Locus of Slaanesh: Add 1 to the Strength characteristic of models in friendly **Slaanesh Daemon** units whilst their unit is within 6" of any units with this ability.
	Scything Impact: After this model finishes a charge move, roll one D6 for each enemy model that is within 1" of this model; for each roll of 5+ that enemy model's unit suffers 1 mortal wound.
PSYKER	This model can attempt to manifest one psychic power in each friendly Psychic phase, and attempt to deny one psychic power in your opponent's Psychic phase. It knows the *Smite* psychic power and one psychic power from the Slaanesh discipline (see *Codex: Chaos Daemons*).
FACTION KEYWORDS	**Chaos, Slaanesh, Daemon**
KEYWORDS	**Character, Chariot, Daemonette, Psyker, Exalted Seeker Chariot, Herald of Slaanesh**

HERALD OF SLAANESH
ON SEEKER CHARIOT

NAME	M	WS	BS	S	T	W	A	Ld	Sv
Herald of Slaanesh on Seeker Chariot	12"	2+	2+	4	5	7	6	8	4+

A Herald of Slaanesh on Seeker Chariot is a single model equipped with: lashes of torment; lashing tongues; ravaging claws.

WEAPON	RANGE	TYPE	S	AP	D	ABILITIES
Lashes of torment	6"	Assault D6	4	0	1	This weapon can be fired even if there are enemy units within 1" of the bearer, and attacks made with this weapon can target enemy units within 1" of friendly units.
Lashing tongues	Melee	Melee	4	0	1	When the bearer fights, it makes 4 additional attacks with this weapon and no more than 4 attacks can be made with this weapon.
Ravaging claws	Melee	Melee	User	-1	2	When resolving an attack made with this weapon, on a wound roll of 6+ this weapon has an Armour Penetration characteristic of -4 for that attack.

ABILITIES	**Daemonic, Quicksilver Swiftness, Daemonic Ritual** (see *Codex: Chaos Daemons*)
	Locus of Slaanesh: Add 1 to the Strength characteristic of models in friendly **Slaanesh Daemon** units whilst their unit is within 6" of any models with this ability.
	Scything Impact: After this model finishes a charge move, roll one D6 for each enemy model that is within 1" of this model; for each roll of 6, that model's unit suffers 1 mortal wound.
PSYKER	This model can attempt to manifest one psychic power in your Psychic phase and attempt to deny one psychic power in your opponent's Psychic phase. It knows *Smite* and one psychic power from the Slaanesh discipline (see *Codex: Chaos Daemons*).
FACTION KEYWORDS	**Chaos, Slaanesh, Daemon**
KEYWORDS	**Character, Chariot, Daemonette, Psyker, Seeker Chariot, Herald of Slaanesh**

HERALD OF SLAANESH
on HELLFLAYER

NAME	M	WS	BS	S	T	W	A	Ld	Sv
Herald of Slaanesh on Hellflayer	12"	2+	2+	4	5	6	5	8	4+

A Herald of Slaanesh on Hellflayer is a single model equipped with: lashes of torment; bladed axle; lashing tongues; ravaging claws.

WEAPON	RANGE	TYPE	S	AP	D	ABILITIES
Lashes of torment	6"	Assault D6	4	0	1	This weapon can be fired even if there are enemy units within 1" of the bearer, and attacks made with this weapon can target enemy units within 1" of friendly units.
Bladed axle	Melee	Melee	x2	-1	2	When the bearer fights, it makes D6 additional attacks with this weapon and no more than that number of attacks can be made with this weapon.
Lashing tongues	Melee	Melee	4	0	1	When the bearer fights, it makes 4 additional attacks with this weapon and no more than 4 attacks can be made with this weapon.
Ravaging claws	Melee	Melee	User	-1	1	When resolving an attack made with this weapon, on a wound roll of 6+ this weapon has an Armour Penetration characteristic of -4 for that attack.

ABILITIES	**Daemonic, Quicksilver Swiftness, Daemonic Ritual** (see *Codex: Chaos Daemons*) **Locus of Slaanesh:** Add 1 to the Strength characteristic of models in friendly **SLAANESH DAEMON** units whilst their unit is within 6" of any models with this ability.
PSYKER	This model can attempt to manifest one psychic power in each friendly Psychic phase, and attempt to deny one psychic power in your opponent's Psychic phase. It knows the *Smite* psychic power and one psychic power from the Slaanesh discipline (see *Codex: Chaos Daemons*).
FACTION KEYWORDS	**CHAOS, SLAANESH, DAEMON**
KEYWORDS	**CHARACTER, CHARIOT, DAEMONETTE, PSYKER, HELLFLAYER, HERALD OF SLAANESH**

FIENDS

2 POWER

NAME	M	WS	BS	S	T	W	A	Ld	Sv
Fiend	14"	3+	-	4	4	4	4	7	6+
Blissbringer	14"	3+	-	4	4	4	5	7	6+

This unit contains 1 Fiend. It can additionally contain up to 8 Fiends (**Power Rating +2** per model). If this unit contains at least 3 models, it can contain 1 Blissbringer instead of 1 Fiend. Every model is equipped with: dissecting claws; vicious barbed tail.

WEAPON	RANGE	TYPE	S	AP	D	ABILITIES
Dissecting claws	Melee	Melee	User	-1	2	When resolving an attack made with this weapon, on a wound roll of 6+ this weapon has an Armour Penetration characteristic of -4 for that attack.
Vicious barbed tail	Melee	Melee	User	-3	D3	When the bearer fights, no more than 1 attack can be made with this weapon.

ABILITIES	Daemonic, Quicksilver Swiftness, Daemonic Ritual (see *Codex: Chaos Daemons*) **Disruptive Song:** When a Psychic test is taken for a model within 12" of any enemy models with this ability, subtract 1 from the total. **Soporific Musk:** Units within 1" of any enemy models with this ability cannot Fall Back unless they can **FLY**.
FACTION KEYWORDS	**CHAOS, SLAANESH, DAEMON**
KEYWORDS	**BEAST, FIENDS**

SEEKERS

4 POWER

NAME	M	WS	BS	S	T	W	A	Ld	Sv
Seeker	14"	3+	3+	3	3	2	2	7	6+
Heartseeker	14"	3+	3+	3	3	2	3	7	6+

This unit contains 1 Heartseeker and 4 Seekers. It can additionally contain up to 5 Seekers (**Power Rating +4**), up to 10 Seekers (**Power Rating +8**) or up to 15 Seekers (**Power Rating +12**). Every model is equipped with: lashing tongue; piercing claws.

WEAPON	RANGE	TYPE	S	AP	D	ABILITIES
Lashing tongue	Melee	Melee	4	0	1	When the bearer fights, it makes 2 additional attacks with this weapon and no more than 2 attacks can be made with this weapon.
Piercing claws	Melee	Melee	User	-1	1	When resolving an attack made with this weapon, on a wound roll of 6+ this weapon has an Armour Penetration characteristic of -4 for that attack.

WARGEAR OPTIONS	• 1 model that does not have an Instrument of Chaos can have a Daemonic Icon. • 1 model that does not have a Daemonic Icon can have an Instrument of Chaos.
ABILITIES	Daemonic, Quicksilver Swiftness, Daemonic Ritual (see *Codex: Chaos Daemons*) **Unholy Speed:** When a charge roll is made for this unit, you can re-roll the dice. **Instrument of Chaos:** If this unit has an Instrument of Chaos, then when an Advance or charge roll is made for this unit, add 1 to the roll.	**Daemonic Icon:** If this unit has a Daemonic Icon, then when a Morale test is taken for this unit, on a roll of 1 it is automatically passed and you can return up to D3 destroyed models from this unit to the battlefield with all of their wounds remaining, placing them in unit coherency (if a model cannot be placed in this way, it is not returned to the battlefield).
FACTION KEYWORDS	**CHAOS, SLAANESH, DAEMON**
KEYWORDS	**CAVALRY, DAEMONETTE, SEEKERS**

HORRORS

NAME	M	WS	BS	S	T	W	A	Ld	Sv
Pink Horror	6"	4+	4+	3	3	1	1	7	6+
Blue Horror	6"	5+	-	2	3	1	1	7	6+
Pair of Brimstone Horrors	6"	5+	-	1	3	1	2	7	6+
Iridescent Horror	6"	4+	4+	3	3	1	2	7	6+

This unit can contain any combination of the following models: Pink Horrors, Blue Horrors, Pairs of Brimstone Horrors. This unit contains 10 models. It can additionally contain up to 10 models (**Power Rating +4**) or up to 20 models (**Power Rating +8**). This unit can contain 1 Iridescent Horror instead of 1 Pink Horror. The Iridescent Horror and every Pink Horror are equipped with: coruscating flames.

WEAPON	RANGE	TYPE	S	AP	D	ABILITIES
Coruscating flames	18"	Assault 2	User	0	1	-

WARGEAR OPTIONS	
	• For every 10 models this unit contains, 1 Pink Horror that does not have an Instrument of Chaos can have a Daemonic Icon.
	• For every 10 models this unit contains, 1 model that does not have a Daemonic Icon can have an Instrument of Chaos.

ABILITIES

Daemonic Ritual (see *Codex: Chaos Space Marines*, *Codex: Thousand Sons* or *Codex: Chaos Daemons*)

Iridescent Horror: An Iridescent Horror counts as a Pink Horror for the purposes of this unit's other abilities.

Split: When a Pink Horror in this unit is destroyed in any phase other than the Morale phase, you can add up to 2 Blue Horrors to this unit before removing that Pink Horror from play. When a Blue Horror in this unit is destroyed in any phase other than the Morale phase, you can add 1 Pair of Brimstone Horrors to this unit before removing that Blue Horror from play. When adding a model to this unit using this ability, it must be placed in unit coherency and more than 1" away from any enemy models (if a model cannot be placed in this way, it is not added to the unit).

Matched Play: Models added to this unit using the Split ability must be paid for with reinforcement points, but can take the unit above its starting size.

Ephemeral Daemons: Pink Horrors have an invulnerable save of 4+. Blue Horrors have an invulnerable save of 5+. Pairs of Brimstone Horrors have an invulnerable save of 6+.

Magical Horde: Whilst this unit contains 20 or more Pink Horrors, the Type characteristic of Coruscating Flames that models in this unit are equipped with is Assault 3.

Psyker Unit: Before manifesting or denying a psychic power with this unit, select one model in this unit to be the source. When manifesting or denying that psychic power, measure distances and, if required, line of sight from that model. If this unit suffers Perils of the Warp, it suffers D3 mortal wounds as described in the core rules, but units within 6" will only suffer mortal wounds if the Perils of the Warp causes the last model in this unit to be slain.

Magic Made Manifest: When a Psychic test or Deny the Witch test is taken for this unit, roll one D6 instead of 2D6. In addition, when this unit manifests *Smite* whilst it contains fewer than 10 Pink Horrors, the closest visible enemy unit within 18" can only suffer 1 mortal wound, irrespective of the result of the Psychic test.

Brimstone Horror: When a Pair of Brimstone Horrors in this unit is selected as the source for manifesting or denying a psychic power, that model is destroyed after that psychic power has been resolved or denied.

Daemonic Icon: If this unit has any Daemonic Icons, then when a Morale test is taken for this unit, on a roll of 1 it is automatically passed and you can return up to D6 destroyed Pink Horrors from this unit to the battlefield with 1 wound remaining, placing them in unit coherency (if a model cannot be placed in this way, it is not returned to the battlefield).

Instrument of Chaos: If this unit has any Instruments of Chaos, then when an Advance or charge roll is made for this unit, add 1 to the roll.

PSYKER	This unit can attempt to manifest one psychic power in your Psychic phase, and attempt to deny one psychic power in your opponent's Psychic phase. It knows *Smite*.
FACTION KEYWORDS	**CHAOS, TZEENTCH, DAEMON**
KEYWORDS	**INFANTRY, PSYKER, HORRORS**

BLOODCRUSHERS

NAME	M	WS	BS	S	T	W	A	Ld	Sv
Bloodcrusher	8"	3+	3+	5	4	4	3	7	4+
Bloodhunter	8"	3+	3+	5	4	4	4	7	4+

This unit contains 1 Bloodhunter and 2 Bloodcrushers. It can additionally contain up to 3 Bloodcrushers (**Power Rating +6**), up to 6 Bloodcrushers (**Power Rating +12**) or up to 9 Bloodcrushers (**Power Rating +18**). Every model is equipped with: bladed horn; hellblade.

WEAPON	RANGE	TYPE	S	AP	D	ABILITIES
Bladed horn	Melee	Melee	User	-1	1	When the bearer fights, it makes 3 additional attacks with this weapon and no more than 3 attacks can be made with this weapon. When resolving an attack made with this weapon in a turn in which the bearer made a charge move, this weapon has a Strength characteristic of +2 for that attack.
Hellblade	Melee	Melee	User	-3	1	When resolving an attack made with this weapon, on a wound roll of 6+ this weapon has a Damage characteristic of 2 for that attack.

WARGEAR OPTIONS	• 1 model that does not have an Instrument of Chaos can have a Daemonic Icon. • 1 model that does not have a Daemonic Icon can have an Instrument of Chaos.

ABILITIES	**Daemonic, Unstoppable Ferocity, Daemonic Ritual** (see *Codex: Chaos Daemons*) **Instrument of Chaos:** If this unit has an Instrument of Chaos, then when an Advance or charge roll is made for this unit, add 1 to the roll.	**Daemonic Icon:** If this unit has a Daemonic Icon, then when a Morale test is taken for this unit, on a roll of 1 it is automatically passed and you can return one destroyed model from this unit to the battlefield with all of its wounds remaining, placing it in unit coherency (if the model cannot be placed in this way, it is not returned to the battlefield).

FACTION KEYWORDS	**CHAOS, KHORNE, DAEMON**
KEYWORDS	**CAVALRY, BLOODLETTER, BLOODCRUSHERS**

FLESH HOUNDS

NAME	M	WS	BS	S	T	W	A	Ld	Sv
Flesh Hound	10"	3+	-	4	4	2	2	7	6+
Gore Hound	10"	3+	6+	4	4	2	2	7	6+

This unit contains 5 Flesh Hounds. It can additionally contain up to 5 Flesh Hounds (**Power Rating +4**), up to 10 Flesh Hounds (**Power Rating +8**) or up to 15 Flesh Hounds (**Power Rating +12**). For every 5 models this unit contains, it can contain 1 Gore Hound instead of 1 Flesh Hound. Every Gore Hound is equipped with: burning roar; gore-drenched fangs. Every Flesh Hound is equipped with: gore-drenched fangs.

WEAPON	RANGE	TYPE	S	AP	D	ABILITIES
Burning roar	8"	Assault D6	4	0	1	When resolving an attack made with this weapon, do not make a hit roll: it automatically scores a hit
Gore-drenched fangs	Melee	Melee	User	-1	1	-

ABILITIES	**Daemonic, Unstoppable Ferocity, Daemonic Ritual** (see *Codex: Chaos Daemons*) **Collar of Khorne:** Once in each of your opponent's Psychic phases, you can select one model in this unit to attempt to resist a psychic power in the same manner as a **PSYKER** by taking a Deny the Witch test. To do so, that model must be within 24" of the enemy model manifesting that psychic power.

FACTION KEYWORDS	**CHAOS, KHORNE, DAEMON**
KEYWORDS	**BEAST, FLESH HOUNDS**

THE INFINITE FORMS OF CORRUPTION

The warp is boundless, time and space irrelevant in the turbulent cradle of Chaos. Though Daemons take on physical forms in realspace that echo the obsessions and desires of their Dark God creators, these are expressed in a myriad of ways. Refracted through the melange of mortal emotions they cause or influenced by the daemonic lord they follow, their variety is infinite.

Contorted Epitome with Mirror of Absorption and coiling tentacles

Striding languidly through its latest arena of desolation, a Keeper of Secrets leads its minions to another promise of orgiastic indulgence among mortal playthings whose emotions are an irresistible lure for Slaanesh's Daemons

Infernal Enrapturess with heartstring lyre

Fiend of Slaanesh with dissecting claws and vicious barbed tail

Syll'Esske, The Vengeful Allegiance

CHAOS DAEMONS STRATAGEMS

If your army is Battle-forged and includes any Chaos Daemons Detachments – that is, any Detachment that includes only units with both the CHAOS and DAEMONS Faction keywords – (excluding Auxiliary Support Detachments), you have access to the Stratagems shown here.

RAZOR-SHARP CARESS
1CP
Slaanesh Daemons Stratagem
Gorging on their prey's emotions, Daemonettes rake their talons through the stoutest armour.

Use this Stratagem in the Fight phase. Select one DAEMONETTE INFANTRY unit from your army. Until the end of the phase, the Armour Penetration characteristic of melee weapons models in that unit are equipped with is improved by 1 (e.g. AP -1 becomes AP -2).

RUST AND DECAY
1CP
Nurgle Daemons Stratagem
Vectors of every contagion from across time and space, Daemon-forged plagueswords are generous to all.

Use this Stratagem in the Fight phase. Select one PLAGUEBEARER INFANTRY unit from your army. Until the end of the phase, when resolving an attack made by a model in that unit, an unmodified hit roll of 6 automatically scores a hit and successfully wounds the target (do not make a wound roll).

SINUOUS UNDULATION
1CP
Slaanesh Daemons Stratagem
Swift beyond mortal comprehension, Steeds of Slaanesh flow like a serpentine blur, near impossible to hit.

Use this Stratagem in your opponent's Shooting phase when a DAEMONETTE CAVALRY unit from your army is chosen as the target of an attack. Until the end of the phase, when resolving an attack made against that unit, subtract 1 from the hit roll.

PUTRID DEMISE
1CP
Nurgle Daemons Stratagem
Nurgle's favoured erupt in a putrid shower upon death.

Use this Stratagem when a PLAGUEBEARER CAVALRY model from your army is destroyed. Before removing that model, roll one D6 for every unit within 6" (excluding NURGLE units). On a 2+, the unit being rolled for suffers 1 mortal wound.

SONG OF DISCORDANT DESPAIR
1CP
Slaanesh Daemons Stratagem
The keening psychic call of hunting Fiends disturbs mental equilibrium, inducing terror and despair.

Use this Stratagem at the start of the Morale phase. Select one enemy unit within 6" of a FIENDS unit from your army. Until the end of the phase, subtract 2 from that enemy unit's Leadership characteristic.

ACIDIC SLOBBER
1CP
Nurgle Daemons Stratagem
With imbecilic affection, Beasts shower their 'friends' in bile so rotten there is soon no distinguishing the victim.

Use this Stratagem in the Fight phase. Select one BEASTS OF NURGLE unit from your army. Until the end of the phase, when resolving an attack made by a model in that unit, an unmodified wound roll of 6 inflicts 1 mortal wound on the target in addition to any other damage.

FLENSING IMPACT
1CP
Slaanesh Daemons Stratagem
Every surface of these dread pain engines is covered in a riot of blades, their merest cut inflicting agony.

Use this Stratagem in the Fight phase. Select one DAEMONETTE CHARIOT unit from your army that made a charge move this turn. Until the end of the phase, when resolving an attack made by a model in that unit, an unmodified hit roll of 6 scores 1 additional hit.

NURGLING INFESTATION
1CP
Nurgle Daemons Stratagem
Nurgle's mites are as numerous as his blessings.

Use this Stratagem at the end of any phase except the Morale phase. Select one NURGLING unit from your army. Roll one D6 for each model in that unit that was destroyed that phase. For each roll of 5+, return one destroyed model to that unit with all of its wounds remaining, placing them in unit coherency (if a model cannot be placed in this way, it is not returned to the battlefield).

RAGE ETERNAL

3CP

Khorne Daemons Stratagem

A rage as limitless as that of Khorne's soldiers overcomes even death's boundary in its intensity.

Use this Stratagem in the Fight phase when a model in a **Bloodletter Infantry** unit from your army is destroyed. Until the end of the phase, roll one D6 each time a model from that unit is destroyed; on a 4+, that model is not removed until after all of the attacking unit's close combat attacks have been resolved, and the destroyed model can make all of its close combat attacks against the unit that destroyed it before being removed (this model can make these close combat attacks even if it would not normally be able to target that unit).

BRASS STAMPEDE

1CP

Khorne Daemons Stratagem

Few things can withstand the thunderous and bloody charge of Khorne's chosen knights.

Use this Stratagem in your Charge phase when a **Bloodletter Cavalry** unit from your army finishes a charge move. For each model in that unit, you can select one enemy unit within 1" of that model and roll one D6; on a 2+, that enemy unit suffers 1 mortal wound; on a 6, that enemy unit suffers D3 mortal wounds. If these mortal wounds destroy all enemy units within 1" of your unit, it can, if you wish, immediately declare another charge.

THE SCENT OF BLOOD

1CP

Khorne Daemons Stratagem

The rich odour of freshly spilled blood will draw loping Flesh Hounds from the foot of Khorne's throne itself.

Use this Stratagem in your Charge phase. Select one **Flesh Hounds** unit from your army. That unit can be chosen to charge with this phase even if it Advanced this turn. In addition, add 2 to the result of that charge roll if any enemy models (excluding **Vehicles**) have been destroyed this turn.

BOUND IN BRASS AND BONE

1CP

Khorne Daemons Stratagem

Khorne's constructs manifest as armour-plated horrors, their dense forms proof against the worst attacks.

Use this Stratagem in any phase when a **Bloodletter Chariot** unit from your army is chosen as the target of an attack. Until the end of the phase, when resolving an attack made against that unit, halve the damage inflicted (rounding up).

MINIONS OF MAGIC

1CP

Tzeentch Daemons Stratagem

Sorcery is intrinsic to the gangling servants of Tzeentch, fate and mutating flames theirs to manipulate.

Use this Stratagem at the start of your Psychic phase. Select one **Horrors Infantry** unit from your army. The first time that unit attempts to manifest a psychic power this phase, do not roll any dice for its Psychic test – instead, assume a 9 was rolled for that Psychic test.

WARP JAWS

1CP

Tzeentch Daemons Stratagem

Burning maws capable of boring through the hull of stranded starships are little hindered by thick hides.

Use this Stratagem in the Fight phase. Select one **Screamers** unit from your army. Until the end of the phase, when resolving an attack made by a model in that unit against a **Monster** or **Vehicle** unit, add 1 to the wound roll.

FLAMES OF MUTATION

1CP

Tzeentch Daemons Stratagem

A cloud of iridescent light or a charred lump of meat – none foresee the fate of those touched by warpfire.

Use this Stratagem in your Shooting phase. Select one **Flamer** unit from your army. Until the end of the phase, when resolving an attack made by a model in that unit, an unmodified wound roll of 6 inflicts 1 mortal wound on the target in addition to any other damage.

WARP PORTAL

1CP

Tzeentch Daemons Stratagem

Like a shimmering patch of wrong sky, a floating doorway disgorges soaring Daemons wreathed in fire.

Use this Stratagem in your Movement phase. Select one **Fluxmaster**, **Fateskimmer** or **Burning Chariot** model from your army. Remove that model from the battlefield and set it back up anywhere on the battlefield that is more than 9" from any enemy models. This model cannot move further this phase.

EXALTED BLOODTHIRSTERS

Vessels of distilled rage drenched in gore, Exalted Bloodthirsters are the greatest servants of the Brass Throne and their lust for battle is exceeded only by Khorne himself. Blessed with murderous rampages of star-spanning violence, wars lead by such Daemons result in oceans of blood and mountains of skulls.

STRATAGEMS

If your army is Battle-forged and includes any Chaos Daemons Detachments (excluding Auxiliary Support Detachments), you can use the Stratagem below.

1CP

EXALTED BLOODTHIRSTER
Khorne Daemons Stratagem

Use this Stratagem before the battle. Select one **BLOODTHIRSTER** model from your army that is not a named character. Until the end of the battle, that model gains the **EXALTED** keyword, and you select one of the Exalted Bloodthirster abilities below for this model for the duration of the battle. Alternatively, you can randomly determine two abilities by rolling two D6 and applying them both to this model for the duration of the battle (if a double is rolled, roll again until two different results are rolled).

EXALTED BLOODTHIRSTER ABILITIES

D6 Result

1 **Hellfire-wrought Armour:** This model has a Save characteristic of 2+.

2 **Blood-blessed:** This model cannot lose more than 8 wounds in the same phase. Any damage inflicted after this point in the same phase has no effect.

3 **Arch-murderer:** Add 1 to the Damage characteristic of all weapons this model is equipped with.

4 **Slaughterborn:** If, in the Charge phase, this model makes a charge move, is charged by any enemy units, or performs a Heroic Intervention, add 1 to its Strength and Attacks characteristics until the end of the following Fight phase. This is cumulative with the Unstoppable Ferocity ability.

5 **Rage Unchained:** This model is considered to have double the number of wounds remaining for the purposes of determining what row to use on its damage table.

6 **Unrivalled Battle-lust:** When a charge roll is made for this model, add 2 to the result. In addition, this model can perform a Heroic Intervention if there are any enemy units within 6" of them instead of 3", and when doing so can move up to 6" instead of 3".

ARTEFACTS OF BLOOD

If your army is led by a Warlord with the **Khorne Daemon** Faction keywords, you can give one of the following Hellforged Artefacts to an **Exalted Bloodthirster** model from your army, instead of giving them a Hellforged Artefact from another source.

G'rmakht the Destroyer

The black blade of this enormous axe contains the essence of G'rmakht, a Bloodthirster whose cyclic imprisonment is an eternal torment. Should the axe's wielder fall, and its death be sufficiently violent, G'rmakht uses its banishment to temporarily unbind its soul-chains, manifesting in the former Daemon's place and venting its unbridled anger upon any it finds before the axe's inescapable power ensnares it once more.

Model with an axe of Khorne only. This Relic replaces an axe of Khorne and has the following profile:

G'rmakht the Destroyer

RANGE	TYPE	S	AP	D
Melee	Melee	+3	-4	D6

Abilities: When resolving an attack made with this weapon, a damage roll of 1 or 2 counts as 3 instead.

In addition, the first time a model with this Relic is destroyed, roll one D6. On a 4+, set that model up again, at the end of the phase, as close as possible to its previous position and more than 1" from any enemy models, with D6 wounds remaining. That model loses all Warlord Traits, Relics and Exalted abilities it had – instead, it always has the Rage Unchained Exalted ability (see left). If the destroyed model was your Warlord, that model is no longer your Warlord, and your Warlord counts as having been destroyed.

Blood-drinker Talisman

This living, rune-etched ruby, swallowed by the Exalted Bloodthirster, has an endless appetite for gore. As the Daemon fells each foe, the talisman boils their blood, reforging the Daemon's flesh as it absorbs every drop.

Roll one D6 each time an attack made with a melee weapon by a model with this Relic destroys an enemy model; on a 5+, the model with this Relic regains 1 lost wound after it has resolved all of its close combat attacks for that fight. A model with this Relic cannot regain more than 8 lost wounds during the same turn as the result of this artefact.

Rune of Brass

Etched into the Daemon's armour – or embedded into its flesh – the Rune of Brass retains the heat of creation, the glare of its still-molten form painful for witches to look upon, their powers twisting against them.

Enemy **Psykers** suffer Perils of the Warp on any Psychic test that includes any double whilst they are within 16" of this model. Enemy **Psykers** that suffer Perils of the Warp whilst they are within 16" of this model suffer 3 mortal wounds (do not roll to determine how many mortal wounds are inflicted).

EXALTED LORDS OF CHANGE

Duplicitous, manipulating and possessing knowledge spanning every time and realm of existence, Exalted Lords of Change ensure the Changer of the Ways' schemes are carried out as intended. They are foci upon which fate turns, terrifying mutators and bewildering magisters far beyond the ken of mortals.

STRATAGEMS

If your army is Battle-forged and includes any Chaos Daemons Detachments (excluding Auxiliary Support Detachments), you can use the Stratagem below.

1CP

EXALTED LORD OF CHANGE
Tzeentch Daemons Stratagem

Use this Stratagem before the battle. Select one **LORD OF CHANGE** model from your army that is not a named character. Until the end of the battle, that model gains the **EXALTED** keyword, and you select one of the Exalted Lord of Change abilities below for this model for the duration of the battle. Alternatively, you can randomly determine two abilities by rolling two D6 and applying them both to this model for the duration of the battle (if a double is rolled, roll again until two different results are rolled).

EXALTED LORD OF CHANGE ABILITIES

D6   Result

1   **Mastery of Magic:** This model knows one additional psychic power from the Tzeentch discipline *(see Codex: Chaos Daemons)* and can attempt to manifest one additional psychic power in each of your Psychic phases.

2   **Spell-thief:** When this model successfully denies a psychic power, the **PSYKER** unit that attempted to manifest that power loses it and cannot attempt to manifest it again this battle.

3   **Lord of Flux:** When an enemy unit suffers mortal wounds as the result of a psychic power manifested by this model, that enemy unit suffers 1 additional mortal wound (e.g. if this model manifested *Smite*, the nearest visible enemy unit would suffer D3+1 mortal wounds).

4   **Nexus of Fate:** If this model is on the battlefield at the start of your turn, roll one D6; on a 1 or a 6 you immediately gain one Command Point.

5   **Aura of Mutability:** When this model would lose a wound as a result of an attack, roll one D6; on a 6 that wound is not lost. After a unit has finished resolving all of its attacks against this model, this model regains one lost wound for each wound it negated because of this ability.

6   **Architect of Deception:** When resolving an attack made with ranged weapon against this model, subtract 1 from the hit roll.

ARTEFACTS OF CHANGE

If your army is led by a Warlord with the **Tzeentch Daemon** Faction keywords, you can give one of the following Hellforged Artefacts to an **Exalted Lord of Change** model from your army, instead of giving them a Hellforged Artefact from another source.

WARPFIRE BLADE

Existing in nine times nine dimensions, the Warpfire Blade flickers with the bearer's sorcerous power. Every iteration of the blade strikes in differing forms and at varying angles – a plane of sharpened will, an outstretched hand of friendship, a wave of stellar fire – seeking through every sub-existence to sever the soul of those it strikes.

Model with baleful sword only. This Relic replaces a baleful sword and has the following profile:

Warpfire Blade				
RANGE	TYPE	S	AP	D
Melee	Melee	+2	-3	D6

Abilities: When resolving an attack made with this weapon, an unmodified wound roll of 6 inflicts D3 mortal wounds on the target in addition to the normal damage.

SOUL-EATER STAVE

Invisible to those without witch-sight, ethereal pseudopods, grasping talons and maws of non-matter surround this twisted staff, ever alert to the cry of a soul newly torn from its body. Riding the power channelled by the staff's bearer, they hungrily devour every scrap of soul-stuff they can catch before it is lost to the maelstrom of the warp's other predators, invigorating the Daemon with stolen vigour.

Roll one D6 when a psychic power manifested by a model with this Relic destroys an enemy model; on a 4+, the model with this Relic immediately regains 1 lost wound. A model cannot regain more than 9 lost wounds during the same turn as the result of this Relic.

THE CRYSTAL TOME

Feared even by many of Tzeentch's servants for its reputed sentience, the Crystal Tome is said by some to contain the true name of every being who might have been, including those who never were. Invoking a creature's true name grants tremendous power over it, yet there have been some known to resist. Whether this is due to a trait of their own or some perversity on behalf of the tome itself may never be known.

At the beginning of your opponent's turn, select one enemy **Character** model within 12" of a model with this Relic. You and your opponent then roll off; your opponent adds the Leadership characteristic of their model to the result, and you add the Leadership characteristic of the model with this Relic to your result. If your total equals or beats your opponent's, then all aura abilities that their **Character** model has cannot be used until the beginning of your opponent's next turn.

EXALTED GREAT UNCLEAN ONES

Mountains of corruption and giants of filth, there are no more bounteous creatures in existence than Exalted Great Unclean Ones, granting Nurgle's gifts with a charitable largesse. Each has successfully led a Plague Legion in every stage of the cycle of virulence, perpetuating and taking lives in their millions.

STRATAGEMS

If your army is Battle-forged and includes any Chaos Daemons Detachments (excluding Auxiliary Support Detachments), you can use the Stratagem below:

1CP

EXALTED GREAT UNCLEAN ONE
Nurgle Daemons Stratagem

Use this Stratagem before the battle. Select one **GREAT UNCLEAN ONE** model from your army that is not a named character. Until the end of the battle, that model gains the **EXALTED** keyword, and you select one of the Exalted Great Unclean One abilities below for this model for the duration of the battle. Alternatively, you can randomly determine two abilities by rolling two D6 and applying them both to this model for the duration of the battle (if a double is rolled, roll again until two different results are rolled).

EXALTED GREAT UNCLEAN ONE ABILITIES

D6 Result

1 **Bloated with Corruption:** This model has a Toughness characteristic of 8.

2 **Revoltingly Resilient:** Add 1 to all Disgustingly Resilient rolls made for this model.

3 **Avalanche of Rotten Flesh:** When a charge roll is made for this model, add 1 to the result. In addition, this model's Crushing Bulk ability inflicts D3 mortal wounds on a 2+, instead of inflicting 1 mortal wound on a 4+.

4 **Living Plagues:** When resolving an attack made with a melee weapon by this model, a successful hit roll scores 1 additional hit if the attack's Strength characteristic is at least twice the target's Toughness characteristic.

5 **Gift of Bountiful Vomit:** In each of your Shooting phases, you can select one enemy unit that is visible to this model and roll one D6 for each model in that unit that is within 12" of this model (to a maximum of 7 dice). For each roll of 3+, that unit suffers 1 mortal wound.

6 **Hideous Visage:** Subtract 1 from the Leadership characteristic of enemy units whilst they are within 12" of any models with this ability from your army (subtract 2 instead whilst they are within 6").

ARTEFACTS OF DECAY

If your army is led by a Warlord with the **NURGLE DAEMON** Faction keywords, you can give one of the following Hellforged Artefacts to an **EXALTED GREAT UNCLEAN ONE** model from your army, instead of giving them a Hellforged Artefact from another source.

EFFLUVIOR

Inside each of the lumpen and pock-marked skulls hanging from the chains of this dread flail lies a portal to the bottomless Marren Mere within the Garden of Nurgle. Into the Mere seeps all the concentrated filth drained from the Garden's limitless bounty and every swing of Effluvior sends out a spray of this flesh-eating and rock-melting soup. Those not crushed by the heavy skulls are left as greasy pools of stinking effluvia.

EXALTED GREAT UNCLEAN ONE with plague flail only. This Relic replaces a plague flail and has the following profile:

Effluvior				
RANGE	TYPE	S	AP	D
7"	Assault 6	+1	-3	2

Abilities: The bearer can make attacks with this weapon whilst within 1" of an enemy unit, and attacks with this weapon can target enemy units within 1" of friendly units. Excess damage from this weapon is not lost; instead, keep allocating damage to another model in the target unit until either all the damage has been allocated or the unit has been destroyed.

TOME OF A THOUSAND POXES

How this rotten volume found its way out of the diseased libraries of the scholar Ku'gath may never be known, but within its wet pages of daemonhide are the secrets of many of the Plaguefather's most ruinous plagues. Even the simplest infection can bloom into new and vibrant potency by using the arcane incantations within its pages, each inscribed in divine ichor.

A model with this Relic knows one additional psychic power from the Nurgle discipline (see *Codex: Chaos Daemons*). In addition, if the unmodified result of a Psychic test taken for a model with this Relic is 7, the psychic power being manifested cannot be denied.

THE ENDLESS GIFT

Waxing strong within Grandfather Nurgle's benevolence, only the truly favoured of the deity's servants are granted the Endless Gift. A disease of such septic and life-giving malignancy, the host's bulging folds of flesh undergo a constant renewal in ever fouler guises. The Endless Gift is granted to those whose own bequests to existence are far too interesting to be allowed to wither away.

A model with this Relic regains one lost wound at the end of each phase in which it lost any wounds.

EXALTED KEEPERS OF SECRETS

Glamour-wreathed, stiletto-clawed and black-hearted, Exalted Keepers of Secrets are the ultimate expressions of every obsession, their sickening presence enough to drive lesser warriors to rapturous seizures. Perverse acts of tortuous intensity are committed with lightning speed and dark glee.

STRATAGEMS

If your army is Battle-forged and includes any Chaos Daemons Detachments (excluding Auxiliary Support Detachments), you can use the Stratagem below:

1CP — EXALTED KEEPER OF SECRETS
Slaanesh Daemons Stratagem

Use this Stratagem before the battle. Select one **KEEPER OF SECRETS** model from your army that is not a named character. Until the end of the battle, that model gains the **EXALTED** keyword, and you select one of the Exalted Keeper of Secrets abilities below for this model for the duration of the battle. Alternatively, you can randomly determine two abilities by rolling two D6 and applying them both to this model for the duration of the battle (if a double is rolled, roll again until two different results are rolled).

EXALTED KEEPER OF SECRETS ABILITIES

D6 Result

1 **Realm-racer:** Add 2" to this model's Move characteristic. When an Advance or charge roll is made for this model, add 1 to the result.

2 **Quicksilver Reflexes:** This model has a 4+ invulnerable save.

3 **Blessing of the Dark Prince:** When resolving an attack made with a ranged weapon against this model, subtract 1 from the wound roll.

4 **Lightning Flayer:** When resolving an attack made with a melee weapon by this model, an unmodified hit roll of 6 scores 1 additional hit.

5 **Fear-seeker:** Once per Morale phase, after an enemy unit fails a Morale test but before any models flee that unit, this model can move as if it were your Movement phase, so long as it ends this move closer to the unit that failed that Morale test. In addition, each time an enemy model flees from a unit whilst its unit is within 6" of this model, this model regains 1 lost wound.

6 **Battle Rapture:** This model can perform a Heroic Intervention if there are any enemy units within 6" of them instead of 3", and when doing so can move up to 6" instead of 3". In addition, each time this Keeper of Secrets consolidates, it can move up to D3+3" instead of 3".

ARTEFACTS OF EXCESS

If your army is led by a Warlord with the **Slaanesh Daemon** Faction keywords, you can give one of the following Hellforged Artefacts to an **Exalted Keeper of Secrets** model from your army, instead of giving them a Hellforged Artefacts from another source.

Silverstrike

The blinding speed with which this blade flicks out makes it appear as if it does not even occupy the space between thrust and strike. In a heartbeat, limbs and heads part from bodies or choice cuts suddenly appear in, marring faces which sag in blissful ignorance.

This Relic replaces a witstealer sword and has the following profile:

Silverstrike				
RANGE	TYPE	S	AP	D
Melee	Melee	+2	-3	3

Abilities: When the bearer fights, it makes 2 additional attacks with this weapon. In addition, subtract 1 from hit rolls for attacks made by a model that has lost any wounds from this weapon.

Whip of Agony

This twitching lash coils lazily and deceptively around its master's limbs, until willed into a serpentine strike. The Whip of Agony exudes a psychic poison, linking its sentience with the nerves of any it touches. With the connection made, the whip's febrile imagination pours pain and horror into the sensorium of its victims.

Model with living whip only. This Relic replaces a living whip and has the following profile:

Whip of Agony				
RANGE	TYPE	S	AP	D
6"	Assault 6	6	-3	2

Abilities: The bearer can make attacks with this weapon whilst within 1" of an enemy unit, and attacks with this weapon can target enemy units within 1" of friendly units. Attacks made with this weapon automatically wound (no wound roll is made) unless the target is a **Vehicle** or **Titanic** unit.

Jewel of Excess

Seeming as one perfect ornament among many worn by the Daemon, the Jewel of Excess is in fact a tormenting prison, housing the souls of every psyker ever slain by the Keeper of Secrets, their power now the Daemon's.

When a model with this Relic takes a Psychic test whilst attempting to manifest psychic powers from the Slaanesh discipline (see *Codex: Chaos Daemons*), add 1 to the result. In addition, when a Deny the Witch test is taken for a model with this Relic, add 1 to the result.

CHAOS DAEMONS NAME GENERATOR

A Daemon takes care to hide its true name, for it can be enslaved by one who speaks it aloud. Most mortals would be rendered insane if they heard them. Yet, like everything of the warp, a Daemon's names are in constant flux and many employ 'use-names', false cognomens they adopt as mood or circumstance dictate.

The tables on these pages allow you to give 'use-names' to your malefic servants. There is no such thing as a typical Daemon, but many go by one or two use-names, each consisting of two or more elements. To randomly generate use-name elements, roll a D66 and consult the appropriate table. To roll a D66, roll two D6, one after the other – the first represents tens, and the second represents digits, giving a result between 11 and 66. To make a name, generate two or more elements and join them together; for example, 'maul' and 'brute' would become Maulbrute. Then generate two more components from the table to create another name, such as Breakspine. Alternatively, simply choose a combination of as many elements as you think fit the Daemon's warped temperament, for many will change them to actively avoid identification.

D66	SLAANESH USE-NAME ELEMENT	D66	NURGLE USE-NAME ELEMENT
11	Pain	11	Dreg
12	Quiver	12	Pox
13	Slash	13	Mucus
14	Carnal	14	Bubo
15	Chew	15	Gnaw
16	Spasm	16	Offal
21	Glut	21	Pus
22	Spike	22	Spittle
23	Tremble	23	Rot
24	Thrash	24	Toad
25	Tongue	25	Bile
26	Rip	26	Blister
31	Sharp	31	Canker
32	Vile	32	Fester
33	Whip	33	Leper
34	Taint	34	Mire
35	Maim	35	Vomit
36	Scratch	36	Filth
41	Stare	41	Glop
42	Thrust	42	Gut
43	Heart	43	Gristle
44	Loathe	44	Wither
45	Tear	45	Spume
46	Lewd	46	Ooze
51	Squeeze	51	Gall
52	Crab	52	Maggot
53	Fiend	53	Sore
54	Gnash	54	Worm
55	Grasp	55	Belch
56	Pierce	56	Bog
61	Sin	61	Blight
62	Flush	62	Moulder
63	Lust	63	Slobber
64	Spoor	64	Spew
65	Venom	65	Wort
66	Claw	66	Foul

D66	KHORNE USE-NAME ELEMENT
11	Grunt
12	Bane
13	Sate
14	Vex
15	Dog
16	Maul
21	Sword
22	Fang
23	Hate
24	Rend
25	Skull
26	Brute
31	Red
32	Blade
33	Death
34	Fist
35	Helm
36	Crush
41	Fire
42	Grim
43	Blood
44	Doom
45	Axe
46	Black
51	Break
52	Dread
53	Fury
54	Spine
55	Kill
56	Slake
61	Ash
62	Beast
63	War
64	Flesh
65	Gore
66	Howl

D66	TZEENTCH USE-NAME ELEMENT
11	Cerulean
12	Mad
13	Gibber
14	Wrack
15	Cackle
16	Flux
21	Ichor
22	Wind
23	Face
24	Grab
25	Loon
26	Pest
31	Rabid
32	Froth
33	Pinch
34	Grin
35	String
36	Eye
41	Twist
42	Blast
43	Foam
44	Whine
45	Chaos
46	Spite
51	Spurt
52	Craze
53	Warp
54	Bend
55	Fate
56	Wail
61	Burble
62	Spittle
63	Flame
64	Curse
65	Change
66	Caper